Hearing Your Own Voice

Hearing Your Own Voice:
A Guide for Personalizing Your Shabbat

ARYEH BEN DAVID

KTAV PUBLISHING HOUSE

HEARING YOUR OWN VOICE: A GUIDE FOR PERSONALIZING YOUR SHABBAT
Aryeh Ben David

Published by
KTAV PUBLISHING HOUSE
527 Empire Blvd
Brooklyn, NY 11225
www.ktav.com
orders@ktav.com
Ph: (718) 972-5449 / Fax: (718) 972-6307

Typeset by Raphaël Freeman, Renana Typesetting
Cover design by Jen Klor
Cover picture by Yoram Raanan

ISBN 978-1-60280-297-1

Manufactured in the United States of America

TO MY PARENTS,
Alan *z"l* and Magda Nemlich,
whose love and support
transcend oceans and worlds.

IN GRATITUDE TO
Julie Frank,
whose friendship and generosity
reflect the qualities of her parents,
Irvin and Sharna.

The Franks exemplified
philanthropic optimism, humility,
and devoted friendship.

THIS BOOK IS DEDICATED TO THE MEMORY OF
Irvin and Sharna,
and our continuing fellowship with Julie.

Contents

EXODUS

Acknowledgments

My love for Shabbat has only grown during the past twenty years since we first published this book. In the first edition, I tried to give over a taste of the depth and beauty of our Shabbat conversations, week after week, with students from the Pardes Institute and Livnot U'Lehibanot – conversations that often lasted long into the night until the glow of our candles waned, leaving us to savor the sweet thoughts in darkness.

Later, the focus of the Shabbat table refocused from our students to our six children. Amid the seemingly endless busyness and multitasking of day-to-day life, during Shabbat we gathered as a family and found our spiritual center. Kabbalists refer to Shabbat as the "secret of oneness," and this was certainly true for us. Shabbat created the space for conversations about struggles, dreams, and aspirations – frustrations and jokes – for sharing food, laughter, and love.

During these last ten *Ayeka* years, our personal family has expanded to include all the dedicated individuals who have helped create and build the organization. I have had the great privilege of working with the "dream team" of Yehoshua Looks, Leora Niderberg, Dasee Berkowitz, Tal Attia, Shira Stern, Ilana Sinclair, and Judith Pieprz. Their wisdom and professionalism have imbued our work with soul and love. They have exemplified what it means to work and live with full humility, compassion, and dedication to a vision beyond their individual achievements.

Without the support, direction, and vision of our *Ayeka* board – David Kahn, Mick Weinstein, Clare Goldwater, Lois Leibovitz, Corey Beinhaker, and Natalie Wasserman – we would never have arrived at this moment.

We are deeply indebted to our key partners – the AVI CHAI, Kohelet, Lippman-Kanfer, Mayberg, Jim Joseph, Sharna and Irvin Frank, and Beker Family foundations – who have made it possible for us to focus and continue our work. A special call out to Julie Frank, our beloved friend, supporter, and inveterate question asker, on each parsha.

Noga Fisher and Emily Wichland lent their magical touch to this text to make it clear and aesthetic.

The first edition of this work was dedicated to my parents. Mom, you are still an inspiration to all of us. Pop, though you are residing in the next world, I see you smiling and bragging to everyone up there about your published son. Means everything.

And most of all, this book is offered with deep gratitude to our children. As Sandra and I watch you bring the gift of Shabbat to your adult lives and families, we relive the countless conversations, laughter, and blessings that our Shabbat table has given to us.

Introduction to the New Edition

This book reflects my own personal educational and spiritual process.

Having learned my *alef-bet* at the age of twenty-two, I became consumed with Jewish learning. There were so many books on the shelves, and I wanted to know them all. For many years I sat day and night, obsessed with acquiring as much knowledge as possible. Questions of personal meaning, personal and spiritual growth were sidelined as I tried to play catch-up in the world of Jewish learning.

After many years, however, I began to notice that something was missing. While I had been filling my mind with Jewish wisdom, my heart was running on empty. While I was intellectually engaged, I remained emotionally disconnected. I was simply not bringing the ideas that I had been learning "down" from my head into my heart, and the impact that they were making on my life was marginal.

This awareness led me to create *Ayeka*, an educational approach that harmonizes the voices of the mind and the soul, making room for the wisdom of Torah to make a transformative impact on our outlooks, actions, and journeys.

For me, this was a complete paradigm shift in my approach to Jewish ideas and books. Learning became an intensely personal, ever-deeper pursuit of spiritual growth. Rather than approaching material with the question, "Can I understand the material?" my query became, "What impact will learning this material have on my life?" Learning had become my springboard for living. As the Gemara in *Kiddushin* 40b states, "Greater is learning when it impels one's actions."

When I first published *Around the Shabbat Table* in 2000, it was without this *Ayeka* lens – and now, when I reread the questions for discussion, I find something lacking. Therefore, in this new edition, I have added a fourth question to each chapter: an open-ended thought aimed at stimulating personal, impactful reflection. These are the questions I call "Becoming": How does this learning impact my life, changing who I will be tomorrow, and the day after, and the day after that?

I like to look at the Torah as a matchmaker, a *shadchan*. The Torah comes to introduce us to someone we desperately want to meet, whom we love dearly but for some reason remains just out of reach. Who is this person? Ourselves – upgraded.

This, to me, is the essence of Judaism: entering into a state of "becoming," continuously pursuing our better selves. Rav Kook, taking it one step further, writes that the work to reveal our best selves is actually the way that we serve God.

Anyone who steps onto the path of "becoming" discovers that our best self is already present deep within: that each of us has an infinite number of better selves just waiting to be expressed. I assert that learning Torah is one of the best vehicles for meeting this person, for unlocking all of the doors behind which he or she is hidden, one after another after another (after another)...

I hope you will read this book together with other people that you care about. It is designed to evoke "soul-talk" – to engender a personal, meaningful, and spiritual conversation that will ultimately enable you to take the next step in your life. From my own journey, I know it is difficult to grow alone, and that we can all benefit from the support of family, friends, and soul mates as we begin to move forward.

My prayer is that this book will be one of the catalysts you need for moving to the next stage of your journey, and that you will take many "next steps" toward revealing your best self.

Introduction to the First Edition

The pace and pressures of the workweek often do not afford us the freedom to discuss essential or personal questions. In his book, *The Sabbath*, Abraham Joshua Heschel described life as a "tempestuous ocean of time and toil in which there are islands of stillness." "The island," he wrote, "is the seventh day, Shabbat, a day of detachment from things, instruments, and practical affairs, as well as of attachment to the spirit."

Yet sometimes the opportunity to reclaim this "island of time" is not fully realized. Sometimes the splendor of Shabbat fades – small talk and sluggish fatigue surround the Shabbat table, instead of engaging dialogue and revitalizing conversation. Despite our best intentions, the lack of time and sufficient resources may preclude in-depth grappling with more significant and meaningful issues.

This book is intended to serve as a springboard for more personally stimulating and meaningful Shabbat conversations. The ideas presented are designed for Jewish adults of all backgrounds and religious denominations. They reflect a philosophy that the Torah belongs to and should be accessible to all Jews, whatever they think or believe, wherever they may be. Each unit can be read directly at the Shabbat table. No prior knowledge or preparation is necessary. In this book, each weekly *parsha* (Torah portion) is divided into three independent sections, one for each of the three Shabbat meals.

The three sections reflect the different moods that characterize each of the three traditional Shabbat meals:

1. The first Shabbat meal (Friday night) focuses on a central theme stemming from the week's *parsha*.
2. The second Shabbat meal (Saturday lunch) discusses a human quality or an aspect of interpersonal behavior that emerges from the *parsha*.
3. The third Shabbat meal (*Seuda Shlishit*) retells an anecdote – historical or fictional – related to an event in the *parsha*.

Each of the three sections for each *parsha* is followed by a series of trigger questions, designed to encourage further reflection around the Shabbat table. The first question is of an intellectual nature and directly explores the section that precedes it. The second question expands on the topic being discussed. The third question is of a personal nature, affording readers the opportunity to internalize and reflect upon the topic of discussion. It reflects the belief that a person's engagement with Judaism and Torah should not be an exclusively intellectual endeavor; rather, it should involve his or her entire being. The fourth question invites us to bring the ideas of the *parsha* into our lives, to be affected and grow personally through our engagement with each portion of the week.

Genesis

My father was extremely well versed medically. His frequent conferences with physicians and his daily visits to the hospital had kept him informed of the most recent medical advances. When the doctor suggested chemotherapy, Father said, "You know as well as I do that chemotherapy for cancer of the pancreas is not effective. All it can do is produce undesirable side effects. If it could prolong life, then I would probably be required by *halacha* to do everything humanly possible to live longer, even if it meant living with distress. However, there is certainly no requirement to subject oneself to a treatment that will cause a great deal of misery and not prolong life." The doctor had to agree that Father was right.

In his conversation with Mother, however, the doctor indicated that chemotherapy might prolong life by perhaps three months. She was adamant. As long as there was anything that could be done, it must be done. Who knows but that during those three months, the long-awaited breakthrough in a cancer cure might come about?

"Foolishness," said Father. But mother would not yield.

One time Father and I were alone, and he said, "You know, to subject myself to the misery of chemotherapy when there is nothing to be gained is ridiculous. But if it is not done, Mother will not be at ease. During our marriage I have done many things for Mother's happiness; if I have the opportunity to do one last thing for her, I will not turn it down."

HEARING YOUR OWN VOICE

1. Why do you think that, in his father's eyes, it was probably impossible to persuade his wife to allow him to forgo the chemotherapy?

2. In creating a home, Jewish law stresses the centrality of *shalom bayit* (peace of the home). In your opinion, do you think that

most breakdowns of *shalom bayit* are of an intellectual or of an emotional nature?

3. What examples of self-sacrifice for the sake of a relationship can you think of?

4. *Ayeka?* Who is the most loving person you know? How do you think you could become a more loving human being?

Vayishlach

Coming Home

After twenty years, Jacob returns home. Twenty years earlier he had fled, with nothing, from his brother Esau. Jacob, the "pure one who dwelled in tents," had stolen his older brother's blessing from their father, Isaac. Esau had vowed to take revenge.

For twenty years Jacob had been plagued by lingering questions: Could he ever go home? Had his brother retained his desire for vengeance? And perhaps most tormenting of all, had he been justified in usurping his brother's blessing?

Jacob sends messengers to his brother Esau, and they return with the troubling report that Esau is approaching with four hundred of his men. Jacob is distraught. Overwhelmed with fear, he divides his camp into two and prays for help. Jacob anxiously waits for the imminent encounter; he waits for tomorrow to come.

What is Jacob thinking? What is he feeling? His whole life has led up to this moment. The Torah describes this moment in the most concise terms: "And Jacob remained alone" (Genesis 32:25). Alone. His whole life passes in front of him. In the midst of his wives, his children, and his camp, Jacob is alone, alone with himself. The next day his destiny will be decided.

And Jacob remained alone, and a man struggled with him until the rising of the dawn. And [the man] saw that he could not defeat him Jacob] ... and he said, "Let me go ..." and he Jacob] said, "I will not release you until you bless me." And [the man] said to him, "What is your name?" and he replied, "Jacob." And [the man] said to him, "Your name will not continue to be Jacob, rather Israel, since you have struggled with God and men and you have prevailed." (Genesis 32:25–29)

Who was this man? Or was this a man at all? Why did they struggle? Why was Jacob's name changed, and why precisely at this moment?

With whom was Jacob wrestling? Perhaps with himself. In the stark loneliness of the night, Jacob was confronting his most difficult issues-issues that, in fact, he may have repressed for the last twenty years.

The Midrash states that "the man" was the ministering angel of Esau. After the confrontation, Jacob calls the place *"P'niel* ('Face of God'), because I [Jacob] have seen God face-to-face and succeeded." Jacob understands that this was a spiritual conflict; the essence of his being struggled with the spirit of Esau. The battle of their natures, originally felt in their mother's womb, has now culminated in the battle of their spirits, of their destinies.

For the first time in his life, Jacob is fighting. Twenty years earlier his mother had dressed him in the clothes of Esau and implored him to impersonate his brother, the hunter. She had conveyed to a reluctant Jacob that, in addition to his spiritual side, he must also learn to act in the often difficult and devious world. She had sent him to Laban, where for twenty years he was thrust into the depths of falseness and deceit. Rebecca, the matriarch, self-sacrificingly imparts to her son that the leadership of the world cannot be entrusted to the likes of Esau or Laban. Jacob must learn to cope with, and ultimately subdue, all the forces that impede the perfection of this world. Jacob must learn to fight.

Jacob's wrestling with the angel reflects that he has undergone an overwhelming personality development. He confronts the angel face-to-face and refuses to relinquish control. After fleeing for twenty years he realizes that he is now ready to confront Esau, no matter how defenseless or outnumbered he may be.

This personality change is accompanied by a change of name. No longer will he be called Jacob, "the one who has supplanted or seized." No longer will he see himself as the one who has taken his blessing in stealth. After twenty years Jacob has come to terms with his acquisition of Esau's blessing. Jacob finally realizes what his mother had understood twenty years before: it is God's desire that he assume both the mantle of the inner, spiritual world, that of "dwelling in tents" (i.e., the tent of Torah) and also that of the outer, physical world, that of the hunter and "the field." He wrestles with Esau's angel, the essence of Esau, and wins.

Jacob's wrestling with the angel and subsequent name change are the fulfillment of the chain of events that began with Rebecca's experience of wrestling in her womb, and God's prophecy to her that she was carrying twins – twins who would always struggle and would become two nations forever in conflict. Her mission became to bequeath to Jacob the tools necessary to combat Esau. His willingness and resoluteness to confront the angel represents Rebecca's ultimate triumph.

Yet a price is paid for this victorious feat. Jacob emerges from his wrestling victorious, but not unscathed. His thigh is injured, and he continues with a limp. The Ramban writes that this is symbolic of the history of the Jewish people. Every generation of persecution recalls Jacob's wound, the limping of the Jewish people, and the price paid for continuing to wrestle and to strive to perfect the world. In the uncompromising and determined battle to overcome the forces that hinder or prevent the moral improvement of this world, we have paid terrible prices in our history. We have prevailed, though often wounded and limping.

HEARING YOUR OWN VOICE

1. After wrestling with the angel, Jacob continues with a limp. Rav Kook writes that often after making a significant decision in life, one's will is temporarily weakened. Why do you think this is so?

2. In order to develop another dimension of his personality, Jacob leaves his home for twenty years. The Talmud states that even a prophet would not be accepted or recognized by the inhabitants of his native city. Why do you think this happens? Why is it sometimes difficult to return to one's home?

3. Have you ever wrestled with yourself?

4. *Ayeka?* Who do you need to stand up to? What advice would you give yourself to help you handle this person?

Shabbat Lunch

Flattery

> *Jacob sent messengers to Esau his brother ... and he commanded them saying, "Thus you should say to my master, Esau: 'This is what your servant, Jacob, wants to tell you: I have sojourned with Laban ... and I have oxen, donkeys and sheep, male and female servants; and I have sent to relate this to my master, so that I may find grace in your eyes."' (Genesis 32:4–6)*

Jacob refers to his brother Esau as "his master." When they finally meet, Jacob bows down seven times in front of Esau. He continually recounts to his brother Esau that the objective of all his actions is "to be granted grace" from him.

Is Jacob being deceitful? Is Jacob, through his words and gifts, his overall obsequiousness, attempting to manipulate Esau, to temper Esau's hostility in a disingenuous way? In short, is Jacob guilty of flattery?

Flattery (in Hebrew, *chanupah*), the conveying of insincere, excessive praise in order to gain the recipient's favor, is harshly condemned in Jewish sources. Earnest compliments and support are essential for the development of a positive self-image. Positive encouragement promotes confidence and is vital for building a strong and determined will. Flattery, on the other hand, because of its insincerity and possible dishonesty, only benefits its giver. Instead of imparting true feelings, the flatterer preys on the vulnerability and insecurity of the receiver and transmits what the receiver would like to hear, rather than what he or she should or truly needs to hear. Psalm 11:9 states that the mouth [words] of a flatterer destroys his or her friend.

The Talmud (*Sotah* 41b) comments, "Rabbi Elazar stated that 'anyone who flatters, even babies in their mothers' wombs curse them.'" Why did Rabbi Elazar select this unusual image to describe the effects of flattery? The babies in their mothers' wombs symbolize the future; their "cursing" reflects their anxiety and disappointment over coming into this kind of world, a world plagued by exploitative self-interest.

The immediate danger of flattery is that the speaker is taking advantage of the listener, manipulating the listener to achieve self-serving goals. Ultimately, in a world rife with flattery, trust and confidence weakens and then eventually breaks down. Recipients regard compliments with uncertainty; every positive word of encouragement is suspected of being tainted with a personal agenda. Flattery thwarts the hope of creating a better universe, the silent prayer of all unborn children. The Talmud states "God abhors the one who speaks words with his mouth while thinking other thoughts in his heart" (*Pesachim* 113b).

The Midrash questions Jacob's behavior, asking, "How could he speak in this way to Esau, calling him his master and bowing down to him?" Isn't this a classic example of flattery? Answers Jacob in the Midrash, "Master of the Universe, I am flattering the evil ones in this world, solely to escape being killed by them." Jacob recognizes the problematic nature of his behavior, that his actions are, in principle, unacceptable. Physical survival remains the sole defense for flattery.

HEARING YOUR OWN VOICE

1. The rabbis of the Talmud disagreed over whether Jacob's attempt to win his brother's favor was justified. Some claimed that Jacob should have ignored Esau, not sent messengers, and simply entered Israel. Others assert that he was justified in his actions. What do you think?
2. What differentiates a compliment from flattery?
3. What kind of relationships or situations do you think are especially conducive to flattery? Have you ever struggled with the temptation to flatter someone?
4. *Ayeka?* When was the last time you put a "spin" on your words and were not completely authentic? What could you have done differently?

Seuda Shlishit

Learning from Thieves and Children

Jacob sojourned with his deceitful brother-in-law, Laban, for twenty years. There, Jacob, the "pure one" (Genesis 25:27), learned how to cope in a world filled with treachery.

The *maggid* (preacher) of Mezritch, one of the Ba'al Shem Tov's primary disciples, noted that one could learn many lessons from a thief. Said the *maggid*:

From a thief, one can learn many valuable principles for life:

- A thief will work even at night;
- If he does not finish what he has set out to do in one night, he devotes the next night to it. He never gives up;
- He will work under the most difficult conditions, enduring cold, rain, and physical hardships;
- He will risk his life for small gains;
- He and those who work with him love and trust one another;
- He is devoted to his trade and would not give it up for any other.

The *maggid* added that one could also learn priceless lessons from the smallest, most simple, of children:

- They are often happy for no particular reason;
- They are never idle, even for a moment;
- If they want something, they demand it vigorously until they get it.

HEARING YOUR OWN VOICE

1. The *maggid* of Mezritch wanted to stress that one can learn something from every person. *Pirkei Avot* (Ethics of the Fathers) 4:1 states: "Who is wise? One who learns from everyone." What does this reflect about the Jewish approach to wisdom? What is the difference between knowledge and wisdom?
2. In light of the previous question, why do you think that the Talmud (*Eruvin* 55a) states that the primary obstacle to wisdom is arrogance? What other obstacles would you note?

3. Which one of the lessons to be learned from the thief or child do you identify with most? Why?

4. *Ayeka?* If you were to be more honest with yourself, what would you say?

_____

Vayeshev

Hatred among Brothers

And his brothers saw that their father loved him [Joseph] more than the brothers, and they hated him and they could not talk with him in peace. (Genesis 37:4)

Do not hate your brother in your heart, you should certainly reprove your fellow human being, and do not bare sin on his account. (Leviticus 19:17)

Are these two verses related? Is the source in Leviticus referring to Joseph and his brothers, hearkening back to an earlier fraternal struggle?

Why did the brothers hate Joseph? Is this simply another example of brotherly hatred in the line of Cain and Abel, Isaac and Ishmael, Jacob and Esau, or are other national or historical elements also involved?

Often we think of Joseph's dreams as the cause for the enmity of the brothers, but a closer look reveals that they despised him even before he related his dreams to them. Why did they hate their brother? The verse simply says, "They saw that their father loved

69

him more" (Genesis 37:4). *More* is the key word. The brothers were loved by Jacob, their father, but Joseph was loved "more." The Talmud (*Shabbat* 10b) prohibits the favoring of one child over another. Every child must be appreciated for his or her unique qualities.

Why did Jacob love Joseph more than the other brothers? How could he have introduced such sibling rivalry into his own home? Had not Jacob himself grievously endured his own brother's hatred, fleeing to escape Esau's wrath? How could he not have learned from his own experience?! The Torah supplies the reason. Jacob loved Joseph more "because he was the son of his [Jacob's] old age"(Genesis 37:3). But was Joseph actually the son of Jacob's old age?! Joseph's younger brother, Benjamin, was the last child born to Jacob, the true son of his old age! The Midrash, therefore, reinterprets the simple meaning of the verse: "Jacob loved Joseph more because Joseph was the son who would support Jacob in his old age." The Midrash implies that Jacob loved Joseph more than the other brothers because he recognized that Joseph possessed leadership qualities that would eventually be fulfilled. Joseph was destined to become a leader. Wherever his fate took him, Joseph inevitably would rise to the top. He would quickly become the most powerful person in Egypt.

Because of these nascent leadership attributes, Jacob gives Joseph a special coat. What does the coat symbolize? The "coat of many colors" resembles a robe, a sign of royalty, of kingship. In effect, this symbolizes the coronation of Joseph.

Immediately after Jacob gives the coat to Joseph, the brothers begin to despise him. They realize that this is not a simple case of chosenness. The gift of the coat is the declaration of a decision – Jacob has decided that Joseph will assume the mantle of leadership in the family. Joseph, to the exclusion of the brothers, has been chosen to determine the direction of the Jewish people for the next generation and the future.

The period of Joseph and his brothers occurs at a precarious juncture in the history of the Jewish people. Until now, in each generation, whenever there had been two brothers, one had been selected to continue the line of the Jewish people and the other son had been rejected. Isaac had been chosen, Ishmael rejected; Jacob chosen, Esau rejected. These are the precedents set by the earlier generations; this is what the brothers must have assumed to be the process for the continuation of the line of Abraham. As soon as Jacob selects Joseph, they understand that they have been rejected. They perceive that their way of viewing the world and their dreams for the Jewish people have been discarded.

Why didn't the brothers talk with Joseph? Why couldn't they have approached their father? Why couldn't they have begun to discuss these issues openly, in a peaceful manner?

A closer examination of the story reveals that, in fact, the brothers did not initiate the animosity between themselves and Joseph. The second verse in our *parsha* states that while he had been shepherding with his brothers, "Joseph brought an evil report to their father"(Genesis 37:2). The air between them had been poisoned.

Why did Joseph speak against his brothers? What did Joseph say? Why did he say it? The Torah does not elaborate. Apparently the content of his evil report is less significant than the fact that he brought it.

Perhaps Joseph's informing on his brothers is merely a symptom of his adolescence, a sign of his immaturity. Or perhaps, like his father Jacob, Joseph already intuits that he possesses exceptional leadership potential. He knows that he should and will be the one directing his brothers. The forthcoming dreams confirm this premonition of his impending sovereignty.

Joseph's challenge will be to emend these immature sensations of power, to resist their inebriating influence. Ultimately, his dilemma will be either to remove the hatred that is in his brothers' hearts or to bear sin on their account.

HEARING YOUR OWN VOICE

1. In our opening verse, the primary caution is against maintaining hatred "in one's heart," keeping it inside. Why would it be less problematic to express one's hatred than to sustain it within?

2. Family relations may be especially prone to strong emotional reactions and hurt feelings. While sensitivity and compassion should always be encouraged, the Talmud (*Pesachim* 113b) cautions against having an "oversensitive" personality. Great praise is offered to one who does not easily become insulted, who forgoes life's "slings and arrows." Why do you think that oversensitivity is considered a personality drawback?

3. Have you ever felt intense sibling rivalry in your family? How were you able to overcome it?

4. *Ayeka?* Do you compare yourself to your siblings and/or other family members? What is one small step you could take to help reduce your comparing?

Shabbat Lunch

Lashon Hara

And Joseph brought an evil report about them [his brothers] to their father. (Genesis 37:2)

The tragic story of Joseph and his brothers begins when Joseph brings an evil report about them to their father, Jacob. The Torah does not reveal the details of this evil report, yet from the expression "evil report"(in Hebrew, *dibah ra'ah*), we can discern that Joseph's words would fall into the category of *lashon hara*, evil or destructive language.

Few human actions are condemned as harshly by the sages

as *lashon hara.* Maimonides writes that it is forbidden to live in a neighborhood in which people habitually speak *lashon hara,* and that it was this crime – in the form of the evil report of the spies – that resulted in the condemnation of the Jewish people to forty years of wandering in the desert and that precluded an entire generation from entering the land of Israel.

What exactly is *lashon hara*? The Talmud set forth the general guidelines of the laws of *lashon hara,* which were then categorized by Maimonides. He lists five categories:

1. Gossip: relaying information for no essential purpose.
2. *Lashon hara*: speaking disparagingly (though truthfully) about another.
3. Slander: speaking falsely about another.
4. A "master" of *lashon hara*: someone who habitually speaks *lashon hara.*
5. A "trace" (*avak*) of *lashon hara*: something that, though not itself *lashon hara,* will provoke *lashon hara.*

Lashon hara includes any form of communication that may negatively affect another person. Thus joking at another's expense, using excuses such as "I wouldn't mind if he or she said that about me" or "I'd say it even if he or she were here," fall within the parameters of speech prohibited because of *lashon hara.* Furthermore, even listening to *lashon hara* is prohibited, for as the Talmud states, *lashon hara* kills three people: the person spoken about, the speaker, and the listener.

Avak lashon hara includes any form of communication that implies or is likely to generate *lashon hara.* Thus expressions such as "he or she has really improved" (by implication, he or she was once less successful), "don't ask me about him or her; I don't want to speak *lashon hara,*" or even "What do you think of him or her?" would be proscribed. Even excessive praise of another or commending someone in the presence of people who do not admire him or her is forbidden, out of concern that it may provoke a negative response. Thus we are responsible not only for our own words but also for any of their consequences.

What is the remedy for *lashon hara*? The Talmud states that there is no way to amend or rectify evil speech. Once words have been uttered, they can never be nullified; they can never be retrieved. The Talmud advises two precautionary measures that will hopefully preclude the speaking of *lashon hara*: (1) Since people are incapable of utterly refraining from talking, they should find worthy subjects for conversation. If possible, people should attempt to occupy themselves with learning Torah. (2) An additional preventative measure against *lashon hara* is for people to try to become more humble and sensitive. Taken together, these two suggestions indicate two of the primary causes for speaking *lashon hara*: (1) not having enough serious ideas or content to discuss, hence resorting to speaking about other people, and (2) not sufficiently recognizing or identifying with the pain inflicted upon others.

In his lifetime, Joseph's suffering that he endured helped him develop greater humility, which engendered a greater sensitivity toward his brothers. Ultimately, at the end of the book of Genesis, he accepts his role of leadership while demonstrating great compassion and love for his brothers: "And Joseph said to them [his brothers], 'Fear not, for am I in the place of God? But as for you, you thought evil against me; but God meant it for good, to bring it to pass this day that masses of people should be saved. Now therefore, fear not, I will nourish you, and your little ones.' And he comforted them, and spoke kindly to their hearts" (Genesis 50:19–21).

HEARING YOUR OWN VOICE

1. In what circumstances would it be advisable to say negative things about another? Is there a difference between confiding in a therapist and confiding in a good friend?
2. How can one prevent listening to *lashon hara*? How can we diminish the amount of *lashon hara* spoken in our presence?
3. Do you know any people in whose presence you would never speak *lashon hara*?
4. *Ayeka?* What triggers you to speak unkindly about others? What piece of advice would you give yourself to help you become more careful with your words?

Seuda Shlishit

The Torn Pillow

A man once went about his community slandering the rabbi. Wherever he went, he spoke of the rabbi's shortcomings and oversights. One day he felt remorse over his behavior and went to the rabbi to beg forgiveness. He indicated that he was willing to do anything to atone for his transgressions.

The rabbi told him to take several feather pillows from his home and go to the highest spot in the town. There, he should cut them open and watch the feathers scatter in the wind. Astonished, the man did as the rabbi had requested.

Returning to the rabbi, the man asked if there were anything else that he needed to do.

"Yes," replied the rabbi. "Now go and gather all of the feathers. Despite your sincere remorse and motivation to repair your past actions," concluded the rabbi, "there is simply no way to rectify the damage caused by your words. It is as possible to retract your words as it will be to recover all of the feathers of the pillows."

HEARING YOUR OWN VOICE

1. Why do you think that rabbis (or other public figures) are especially inviting targets for *lashon hara*?
2. What do you think are the most common character traits or circumstances that motivate the speaking of *lashon hara*?
3. What advice would you have given to the man who spoke *lashon hara*? To a friend who speaks *lashon hara*?
4. *Ayeka?* Do you need to be more careful in how you speak about rabbis and Jewish leaders?

Mikketz

The Lesson of Dreams

And it came to pass at the end of two years, that Pharaoh dreamed.... (Genesis 41:1)

Where do dreams come from? Why do we dream? The rabbis asserted that dreams were the last traces of prophecy, the hints of a heavenly encounter.

Three sets of dreams cross Joseph's path. The first set he dreams in his father's house. The second set is dreamed by the butler and the baker while Joseph is confined in Pharaoh's prison. The third set is dreamed by Pharaoh himself, at the beginning of this week's *parsha*.

Why is Joseph's life continually distinguished by dreams? What is the development in this sequence of dreams and in Joseph's responses to them?

In last week's *parsha*, the first set of dreams occurs while Joseph is a seventeen-year-old youth, the favored son of his father, Jacob. Oblivious to the growing friction between himself and his brothers, Joseph calls to them: "Hear this dream which I have dreamed:

77

'Behold, we were binding sheaves in the field and, behold, my sheave arose and stood upright and, behold, your sheaves stood around mine and bowed down to my sheave'" (Genesis 37:6–7).

The reaction of the brothers to Joseph's first dream is eminently predictable: "And the brothers hated him even more, on account of his dreams and his words" (Genesis 37:8). It is understandable that they resent him for the content of his dreams, for the dreams clearly depict Joseph's future dominance over them. But in addition, they hate him for "his words," his untempered arrogance: "Hear this dream which I have dreamt." In an almost defiant fashion, Joseph seems self-absorbed over his impending status of greatness. In Joseph's eyes, the dreams reflect his sovereignty, which he may exploit however he so chooses.

Joseph focuses only on what the dreams portend for him. He ignores their origin as a message and gift from an unknowable source. Joseph continues to disregard the reactions of his brothers and presumptuously reports to them a second dream implying his impending superiority – eleven stars bow down to him. This time he incurs the wrath of his father as well.

There is a Talmudic dictum that God responds to "all those who seek to elevate themselves in their own eyes by humbling them." Accordingly, instead of ascending to power, Joseph is continually thrust downward – down to the pit that his brothers threw him into, down to Egypt, and finally down to the dungeon.

There in the dungeon he is called on to interpret a second set of dreams. Now he responds differently. When approached by the butler and baker to interpret their dreams, Joseph replies, "Do not interpretations belong to God?" Joseph's suffering has diminished his pride. He now understands that God is the source of the dream. No longer absorbed with his own powers of dream interpretation, Joseph now regards himself as a medium, a person capable of providing greater insight and understanding.

Joseph correctly interprets the dreams of the butler and the baker yet does not merit release from his state of suffering. He beseeches the chief butler to mention him to Pharaoh but to no avail – the butler forgets him. For two more years he languishes in the dungeon of Pharaoh, helplessly awaiting salvation.

Finally, "And it came to pass at the end of two years, that Pharaoh dreamed...."

Pharaoh dreams his dreams and summons Joseph to interpret them for him. Two years have elapsed. Joseph realizes that the butler did not implement his release but rather that dreams are determining his fate.

Joseph's response to Pharaoh's dreams is thoroughly unlike his reaction to his own dreams twenty-two years earlier. When asked to interpret Pharaoh's dreams, Joseph first says: "It is not up to me" (Genesis 41:16). He no longer focuses on himself; he no longer attends exclusively to his own well-being. During his dialogue with Pharaoh, Joseph repeatedly states that the dream is what "God has shown Pharaoh to do." Joseph has finally recognized that a dream is God's transmitting of a responsibility; it is less a special privilege than a task with which one has been charged.

The series of dreams that Joseph encounters serve as his education. He is clearly graced with natural powers of leadership, and the dreams of his youth foresee a future endowed with influence and power. The danger lies in his potential conceit.

Joseph, through suffering and tragedy, learns the lesson of humility. Originally blinded by his own exceptional potential, he comes to perceive that these powers are indeed gifts and bring with them responsibility. When Joseph finally reveals himself to his brothers once he has become the vizier of Egypt, his tone bears none of his original haughtiness: "And Joseph said to his brothers, 'Please come near to me.... I am Joseph your brother whom you sold to Egypt. Now therefore be not grieved, nor angry with yourselves, that you sold me here, for God did send me before you to preserve our lives'" (Genesis 45:4–5).

HEARING YOUR OWN VOICE

1. According to Jewish law, one who takes upon him a vow not to sleep for three days is forced by the community to annul his vow and sleep. Why is sleep so vital?

2. Exceptionally talented people often have difficulty relating to others who do not share their ability. What is the lesson of Joseph regarding the most effective way to realize extraordinary potential?

3. Rav Kook writes, "The great dreams are the foundation of the world." What is your most memorable dream – while asleep? While awake?

4. *Ayeka?* Is there a seventeen-year old egocentric voice within you? How do you respond to it?

Shabbat Lunch

Giving a Name

> *And Pharaoh said to Joseph, "Behold, I have placed all of Egypt under your control." And Pharaoh removed his ring from his hand and placed it upon the hand of Joseph, dressed him in clothes of silk and placed a band of gold on his neck ... and Pharaoh called Joseph "Tzafnat Paneach...."* (Genesis 41:41–45)

Why did Pharaoh change Joseph's name? What is the significance of a name'? What does it mean to change a name?

Many figures in the Torah had their names changed. Abram became Abraham. Sarai became Sarah. In both cases, the name changes were final; they were never again referred to as Abram or Sarai. Jacob's name was changed to Israel, though he continued to be called Jacob as well. Later on in the Torah, Moses' disciple and successor Hoshea Bin Nun will have his name changed to Yehoshua (Joshua). Of all the personalities of the Torah, however, perhaps Joseph was the recipient of the greatest number and variety of names.

Rachel, Joseph's mother, gave him a name reflecting two diverse qualities. "She became pregnant and bore a son, saying 'God has taken away [*asaf*] my shame.' And she called him Joseph, saying, 'God will add [*Yosef*] another son to me'" (Genesis 30:23–24). Rachel's first expression – *asaf* – implies a concluding (*sof*) of her misery, while her second expression – *Yosef* – reflects hope and the yearning for a second son. Joseph will both bring an end to suffering (via supplying Jacob and the other sons with food during the famine) and serve as a springboard for a succeeding stage (eventually yielding his leadership to that of Judah).

Joseph's brothers, while plotting to slay him, apparently cannot bear to call him by his given name and refer to him pejoratively as "that dreamer" (Genesis 37:19). While he is in the dungeon, the Egyptian butler refers to him as "the Hebrew slave" (*eved ivri*) (Genesis 41:12). Pharaoh calls him *Tzafnat Paneach* (the revealer of the hidden). In the Talmud (*Yoma* 25b) and throughout Jewish history he is referred to as *Joseph HaTzaddik*, Joseph the righteous.

What is the meaning of a name?

A name is the primary social device of human interaction, the meeting place between the individual and society. First of all, the name should reveal some of the individual's essential character to others. Thus the name bestowed should ideally provide some insight into the true nature of the individual. In the Garden of Eden, Adam's first task was to name the animals, to give them external labels that reflect their innermost beings. In the Talmud, Rabbi Meir attempted to detect some aspect of a person's nature from his or her name; he presumed that a name served as an invaluable guide, reflecting the person's hidden nature (*Yoma* 83b). For parents, the choice of a name is one of the first crucial moments in child rising.

Every human being possesses a unique and ultimately unknowable essence. In the eyes of Judaism, the greatest challenge in life is to acquire greater insight into what this unique gift is and then to understand how to channel and direct these qualities to create a better society. One's name, if properly bestowed, is the first clue in understanding what this character or gift may entail. The name changes of Abraham, Sarah, and Jacob/Israel were God's most poignant messages to them that they must begin to regard themselves differently; they have undergone qualitative changes and must now begin developing and presenting to the world heretofore untapped aspects of their personalities.

Second, a society confers a name to every individual, an appellation reflecting how others regard the most essential aspects of his or her identity. In the Mishnah in *Pirkei Avot*, Rabbi Shimon Bar Yochai states that "a good name" is more valuable than wisdom, holiness, or power. Rabbi Shimon said: There are three crowns: the crown of Torah, the crown of priesthood, and the crown of royalty; but the *crown of a good name* exceeds them all (*Avot* 4:17). Ultimately the name that the world gives to a person, that is, his or her reputation, reflects his or her most significant and lasting contribution.

The many names of Joseph reflect his process of growth and transformation. His special gift of experiencing and understanding dreams undergoes a metamorphosis. Once perceived negatively as "that dreamer," he is ultimately exalted by Pharaoh as "the revealer of the hidden." Eventually Jewish history will bequeath upon Joseph the most valued of all names: *Joseph HaTzaddik*.

HEARING YOUR OWN VOICE

1. The protagonist of Franz Kafka's classic *The Trial* was never given a name. He was referred to simply as "K." Conversely, commentators write that God has an infinite number of names. What do you think these two ideas represent?
2. What is the significance of having, or not having, a Hebrew

name? What "name" would you like, ideally, for others to give to you?

3. What names would you like to give to your children? Why?
4. *Ayeka?* What small step could you take to better merit the "crown of a good name"?

Seuda Shlishit

The Holy Goat

This week's *parsha* spoke of thin and fat cows. Other animals have also played a role in Jewish history and thought.

The following is a story told by Rabbi Mendel of Kotsk (1787–1859), known as the "Kotsker Rebbe." "The "Kotsker" was renowned for his unqualified passion for truth, his unyielding resoluteness to serve God without any personal concern or gain. "Everything in the world can be imitated except truth. For truth that is imitated is no longer truth." Unlike other Hasidic leaders who were known for their unconditional love for all Jews and who attracted wide followings, the Rebbe of Kotsk's zealous fury terrified the few Hasidim who dared to enter his circle. His presence served as a continual reminder for the Jewish people of the ability to strive, without compromise, toward a more sanctified life. During the last years of his life he retreated into seclusion, unable to face the shallowness and hypocrisy endemic to a human world. The following story reflects how he perceived his role amidst his Hasidic followers:

> Rabbi Isaac of Vorke was one of the very few who were admitted to Rabbi Mendel during this period. Once he visited Kotzk after a long absence, knocked, entered Rabbi Mendel's room, and said in greeting: "Peace be with you, Rabbi."
>
> "I am no rabbi! Don't you recognize me! I am the goat! I'm the sacred goat. Don't you remember the story?

"An old Jew once lost his snuffbox made of horn, on his way to the *Beit Midrash* (house of study). He wailed, 'Just as if the dreadful exile weren't enough, this must happen to me! Oh my, I've lost my snuffbox made of horn!' And then he came upon the sacred goat. The sacred goat was pacing the earth, and the tips of his black horns touched the stars. Whenever the goat moved its horns, the most heavenly music resonated from the moving of the stars. When he heard the old Jew lamenting, he leaned down to him, and said, 'Cut a piece from my horns, whatever you need to make a new snuffbox.' The old Jew did this, made a new snuffbox, and filled it with tobacco. Then he went to the *Beit Midrash* and offered everyone a pinch of snuff. They snuffed and snuffed, and everyone who snuffed it cried, 'Oh, what wonderful tobacco! It must be because of the box. Oh, what a wonderful box! Wherever did you get it?' So the old man told them about the sacred goat. And then one after another they went out and looked for the goat.

"The holy goat was pacing the earth and the tips of his horns were touching the stars, conducting the celestial symphony. One after another they went up to him and begged permission to cut off a bit of his horns. Time after time the sacred goat leaned down to grant their request. Box after box was made and filled with snuff. The fame of the boxes spread far and wide. At every step he took, the sacred goat met someone who asked for a piece of his horns.

"Now all the Jews have special snuffboxes to fill their noses with snuff. And the holy goat still paces the earth. But there is no more heavenly music. His horns no longer reach the stars."

HEARING YOUR OWN VOICE

1. What does this story say about the awareness or priorities of people who were solely concerned with their snuffboxes? Why

do you think the goat was willing to sacrifice its horns? Should the goat have consented to sacrifice its horns?

2. The Talmud states that one who purifies those who are impure becomes impure in the process. Those who heal others may often pay a price for their efforts. Why do you think this is so?

3. According to the Kabbalah Jewish mysticism, to enable someone else to grow, one must contract (*tzimtzum*) him- or herself to create space for the other to expand. Have you ever "contracted" yourself in order to create or maintain a relationship?

4. *Ayeka?* What would you say is the most precious gift you could give to others? Can you think of a way in which you could make it even better?

Vayigash

Reconciliation

> *And Joseph could not control himself ... and he raised his voice in crying that was heard in all of Egypt and the house of Pharaoh. And Joseph said to his brothers, "I am Joseph. Is my father still alive?" But his brothers were not able to answer him because of their shock.* (Genesis 45:1–3)

For twenty-two years Joseph had not revealed his identity to his brothers and father. For twenty-two years, Jacob had inconsolably mourned his favorite son, while the brothers bore witness to their father's grief and suppressed their guilt over selling Joseph to Egypt. For twenty-two years Joseph had controlled himself, never sending word of his fate, never seeking to relieve his family's pain.

But now, finally, in one earth-shattering moment, he can no longer control himself. "I am Joseph."

We have to try to understand two questions: What motivated Joseph to conceal himself, and what finally prompted him to reveal his identity to his brothers?

One clue to Joseph's secrecy appeared in last week's *parsha.* "And Joseph saw his brothers and recognized them, but he made himself unrecognizable to them and spoke harshly with them.... And Joseph remembered the dreams which he had dreamt about them, and said to them, 'You are spies...'" (Genesis 42:7, 9). Joseph does not remember "his dreams," rather "the dreams." As Joseph had already told the baker, the butler, and Pharaoh, Joseph understood that dreams came as messages from God. He identifies them as traces of prophecy, which he is forbidden to ignore. Joseph's dream of the stars bowing down to him was finally being realized; the brothers had just bowed down to him. Yet something was missing – here there were only ten brothers, while he had envisioned eleven stars bowing down to him. To completely bring the dreams to fruition, Joseph must devise a family intrigue that will ultimately bring his brother Benjamin, the eleventh star, down to Egypt.

Yet despite the fulfillment of the dreams, Joseph still does not reveal himself to his brothers. Apparently, an additional factor contributes to Joseph's hiding of his true identity.

What finally brings Joseph to reveal his identity? Judah's speech. Immediately after Judah's dramatic monologue at the opening of this week's *parsha*, Joseph realizes that he no longer needs to disguise himself. With a screaming cry that is heard throughout Egypt, Joseph releases twenty-two years of isolated suffering. His superhuman control is no longer necessary. Joseph breaks down in an outpouring of love and compassion for his brothers. They are stunned. How could the one who has tormented them, ridiculed them, and compelled them to jeopardize their youngest sibling Benjamin, now proclaim his love for them? What could have motivated him?

What would have happened if Joseph had immediately revealed himself to his brothers upon their arrival in Egypt? They would forever have berated themselves over their mistreatment of him. They would never have been able to absolve themselves of their sin; they could never have redeemed themselves. Their guilt would have precluded any possible family reconciliation.

Joseph, the original cause of the family dissension, will ultimately become the force enabling their reunion. Joseph carefully engineers the scenario through which Judah is able to atone for the sin of the brothers. Judah, the very brother who proposed to sell Joseph to the Ishmaelites, now emerges as Benjamin's defender and savior. Judah is now willing "to sell himself into slavery" in order to save Rachel's second and only other son, Benjamin. His emotional plea to Joseph to take him into slavery, and release Benjamin, confirms his complete turnaround. Joseph, having enabled Judah and the brothers to exonerate themselves, has nothing left to prove. He collapses with a cry of release, a cry of joy, a cry of freedom.

The confrontation between Joseph and Judah is understood by the rabbis to have eschatological implications. This is not only a struggle between two individuals but between two forces in history. The "end of days" will be ushered in by the succession of two messiahs: *Mashiach ben Yosef* (Messiah as the son of Joseph) and *Mashiach ben David* (Messiah as the son of David, a descendant of Judah). Like Joseph, who provided food during the famine, *Mashiach ben Yosef* will foster the physical prosperity of the Jewish people. *Mashiach ben Yosef* will ultimately yield to *Mashiach ben David*, who will lead the Jewish people into an epoch of internal, spiritual fulfillment.

The rabbis state that the final Messiah will be a descendant of Judah because of Judah's ability to change, to atone for his prior mistake, to recognize his faults and amend his ways.

HEARING YOUR OWN VOICE

1. Following Joseph's revelation of his identity, the Torah states that "And afterward his brothers spoke with him [Joseph]" (Genesis 45:15), though it does not detail the content of their conversation. Why are the details of their conversation less significant than the mere fact that they were communicating? Why is this a fitting end to their crisis?

2. In his eulogy at the funeral of Theodor Herzl, Rav Kook referred to Herzl as a spark in the line of "Mashiach ben Joseph." Why do you think that he said this?
3. What do you think usually prevents family members from reconciling conflicts?
4. *Ayeka?* What relationship in your life is still waiting for reconciliation?

Shabbat Lunch

Giving and Taking Advice

And Judah drew near to him [Joseph] and said, My master, please let your servant speak a word in my master's ears, and do not be angry at your servant, because you are just like Pharaoh. (Genesis 44:18)

At the end of last week's *parsha*, *Mikketz*, after the stolen silver goblet had been found in Benjamin's belongings, Judah offered to indenture himself and all the brothers to Joseph. Joseph refused his proposition, stating, "the man in whose hand the goblet was found shall become my servant, and the rest of you may peacefully return to your father" (Genesis 44:17). Judah then changes his tone, takes the liberty of approaching Joseph, and courageously admonishes Joseph, presently the second most powerful figure in Egypt. In one of the longest speeches in the Torah (seventeen verses), Judah attempts to convince Joseph to change his mind and not subject Benjamin to servitude.

Was Judah obligated to intervene on behalf of his brother, Benjamin?

One of the most crucial, difficult, and hazardous mitzvot in the Torah is the obligation of *tochacha*, understood either as rebuking or giving advice. A Jew is not allowed to idly observe another's behavior; we are actors on the world stage, not spectators. Rabbi Yochanan states in the Talmud, "Anyone who could possibly have prevented another from transgressing and does not prevent it will eventually receive the punishment for that sin" (*Shabbat* 54b). In his epic work the *Mishneh Torah* (Laws of Knowledge 6:6–7), Maimonides codifies and extends this principle:

1. When a person hates another person, he should not despise him in silence ... rather it is incumbent upon him [the hater] to talk to the one he hates and say, "Why did you do this to me? Why did you transgress against me in this matter?"
2. Someone who notices that his friend has sinned, or is not going on a beneficial path, is obligated to return his friend to a better way and to inform him that he is sinning against himself through his actions.

We are obligated not only to prevent someone from sinning but also to prevent one from straying from "a beneficial path." What is this beneficial path? Who is to decide exactly what it is?

Maimonides, always precise in his language, alters the relationship in question in these two laws. The first law, pertaining to the more objective act of "transgressing," concerns "another person," whereas the second law, describing this "beneficial path," deals in the context of a "friend." Precisely because of the depth and trust of the relationship, one bears a special responsibility toward one's friends. This responsibility means not only to be the voice of love and support but also to counsel and, on occasion, to criticize a friend's behavior. To refrain from involvement is regarded as being negligent in the duty and true concern of friendship. It is virtually impossible for one to objectively assess one's own life; one's friends fulfill the critical role of providing greater clarity and insight.

Yet isn't there a great risk involved here? Can't the most well-intended advice sometimes backfire and endanger the strength or very existence of a relationship? Is every piece of advice worth articulating?

Rabbi Ellah said, "Just as a person is commanded to say something which will be heard, so too he or she is commanded *not* to say something which will *not be* heard" (*Yevamot* 65a). The goal is not for the friend to offer advice but to improve the situation. Over two thousand years ago, the Midrash lamented the precariousness of this endeavor:

> Rabbi Tarfon said: "I swear that there is no one in this generation who is worthy of giving someone else advice."
>
> Rabbi Elazar ... said: "I swear that there is no one in this generation who is capable of receiving advice."
>
> Rabbi Akiva said: "I swear that there is no one in this generation who knows how to offer advice."

Prior to delivering words of advice, the individual must examine three elements of the procedure: (1) Am I worthy of offering advice? Is the advice sincere and not stemming from any anger or conceit; could I be accused of being hypocritical? (2) Is my friend capable of accepting the advice? Will he or she become defensive; is he or she feeling secure enough at this time? (3) Is the style and method of giving advice appropriate? If one cannot respond positively to these questions, then one is obligated to remain silent.

Judah's reproof of Joseph serves as a classic example of successfully fulfilling the three components of giving advice. His brave act precipitates the family's ultimate reconciliation.

HEARING YOUR OWN VOICE

1. What are the major obstacles or qualities that preclude the receiving of advice? What eventually happens to a person who is incapable of accepting advice?
2. What usually happens to a relationship when appropriate advice is offered and accepted? How might one overcome the hesitancy of giving advice?

3. Have you ever given or received advice that ultimately deepened the relationship? When?
4. *Ayeka?* What holds you back from receiving advice from others? How could you become more open and receptive to listening?

Seuda Shlishit

A Scratch on the Crown

In our *parsha*, Judah acknowledges and repents for his past mistakes. Twenty-two years after he had suggested selling Joseph into slavery, he defends Joseph's brother Benjamin and offers to take his place as a servant to the Pharaoh of Egypt. His awareness of his previous failings enables him to grow, confront Joseph, and ultimately emerges victorious.

The Maggid of Dovno (1741 1804) was renowned for his moralistic stories. The following story echoes the theme of this week's *parsha*:

> Once, a king owned a great diamond. It was his prize possession, as it had no equal in the world. But one day, he noticed that the diamond had become chipped. Stretching from this chip was a scratch on the diamond – a very deep and jagged scratch. The diamond was no longer perfect. The king despaired.
>
> He consulted all his experts, diamond cutters, and artists. They told him that it was impossible to repair the diamond. One offered to cut off the section that was damaged, but the king did not wish to shrink his precious diamond. One said that the king would simply have to look for a new diamond – for this one was irreparably flawed, but the king did not want to part with his diamond.

Then one day a new diamond cutter came to the kingdom. He had heard about the king's problem and offered to fix the diamond. He said that he could make it look even more beautiful than before.

So the king entrusted him with the diamond, and the new diamond cutter secluded himself in his workroom. For days he did not emerge, his light remaining on all night. How could he repair the chipped and scratched diamond?

Finally he appeared. With a triumphant expression upon his face, he approached the king and presented the diamond, resting upon a scarlet cushion. The king looked and then smiled. He saw what the diamond cutter had done. There sat the diamond, the most beautiful diamond in the world.

In the place of the chip, the diamond cutter had engraved a rose; out of the long and jagged scratch the diamond cutter had carved the stem of the rose.

HEARING YOUR OWN VOICE

1. What light might this story shed on dealing with moments of despair?
2. Moses requested to see the "face of God." God responded by saying that Moses could see "His back." Rav Soloveitchik explains that this enigmatic section of the Torah refers to God's role in history. We cannot understand the "face of God," how God functions in the present, though sometimes when we look "back" in history, hundreds of years later, we can begin to fathom why certain events occurred. Can this idea be connected to the Maggid of Dovno's story?
3. Have you ever profited from a difficult experience?
4. *Ayeka?* What "scratch" in your recent life could you reframe and "turn into a rose"?

Vayechi

Dying Words

The *parsha* of *Vayechi* concludes the book of Genesis. Twenty-three generations after the creation of the world, the human race seems immeasurably removed from its original state. We have moved from the paradise of the Garden of Eden to the spiritual abyss of Egypt. Irrevocably distant from the original world of endless life, the book of Genesis now closes with the embalming of Joseph. Even his physical body is prevented from returning to the cycle of life, "from dust to dust," and now exists in a state of continuous, ceaseless, perpetual death.

The hope of either regaining or recreating paradise has become increasingly remote. The visions and sacrifices of the forefathers have seemingly disappeared as internecine strife plagues the family of Jacob. In the depths of Egypt, amid the impending emergence of a wicked Pharaoh and generations of enslavement, the *parsha* of *Vayechi* renews the hope and vision of the Jewish people.

The centerpiece of the *parsha* of *Vayechi* is Jacob's blessing of his twelve sons. On his deathbed, Jacob gathers all his sons to hear his final words. Each son receives his own individual blessing, without competition, without comparison. Yet it is not clear what Jacob's motivation is for this last dramatic act. What is the nature and purpose of these blessings? Why does Jacob feel a need to bless each of his sons? What is Jacob's intention?

Several questions must be addressed:

1. In the beginning of this *parsha*, Jacob blesses Joseph's children, Efraim and Menashe. Why does Jacob bless his grandchildren before he blesses his own children?! Joseph's children receive a blessing from their grandfather before Joseph receives his own blessing from his father! Why?
2. Jacob begins his blessings with a unique preamble: "Gather yourselves together, that I may tell you that which will befall you in the end of days"(Genesis 49:1). Why does Jacob mention "the end of days?"
3. Why does Jacob first entreat Joseph (Genesis 47:30) and then again command the rest of his sons (Genesis 49:29) to bury him in Israel? Both before and then immediately after the blessings, Jacob returns to this theme of not burying him in Egypt. Why the emphasis and repetition?

Jacob's actions indicate a penetrating awareness of the fragility and potential crisis that the nascent Jewish people may undergo at the moment of his death. First of all, it is critical that he, the last of the forefathers, unite his sons in a bond of mutual cooperation and dependence. There must be an immediate halt to internal dispute; otherwise, the Jewish people are liable to fracture into contentious, vying sects, determined to destroy each other. In order to rectify this problem, Jacob not only gives each of his sons his own unique blessing, but does so *in the presence of all of the other sons.* Each son hears the others' blessings. Each son now realizes that everyone has received a special blessing, that none are competing with or threatening the others' portions. Moreover, the destinies of the brothers are all now interlinked, their futures all mutually dependent.

Unity, however, is not enough. The sons must also be reminded of their ultimate responsibility and purpose.

The next generations of Jews who will be raised in Egypt will be completely different from that of Abraham, Isaac, Jacob, and his sons. These first four generations all lived in Israel. They all benefited from Abraham's historic journey and viscerally experienced the spiritual power of living and walking in Israel. Now, for the first time in its history, the Jewish people face the predicament of assimilation into a foreign culture, in a foreign land. The next generations of Jews will live and die outside of the Promised Land, never having tasted what the Talmud refers to as "the air of Israel, the air that makes one wise."

Thus Jacob directs his sons toward the future. Jacob's first goal is to remind them not to forget that they have a mission extending far beyond himself or herself, that they are essential links in a chain that must continue well after their demise. They must not become consumed with their present life; they must not become enamored of the luxury and modernity of Goshen (their place of abode within Egypt).

To this end, Jacob begins by blessing the grandchildren, Ephraim and Menashe. First and foremost, Joseph (and all the sons through him) must become future-oriented. The blessing for the present only has meaning insofar as it will be sustained in future generations. Similarly, when Jacob gathers together his sons he does not simply offer them his blessing. Rather, he instructs them to reflect upon "the end of days." He wrests them away from the present, engaging them with visions of hope and of their greater, ultimate destiny.

Similarly, Jacob emphasizes and repeats his wish to be buried in Israel. One last time, before they sink into the quagmire of Egypt, the sons must again walk in Israel. Jacob's dying wish is to be buried "with his fathers ... [in the burial site] which Abraham bought." One last time, he reminds them of their past, of their history. Jacob uses the blessings to eternalize his mission and that of his sons, to cogently convey to his sons their role in the fulfilling of this dream.

In Jacob's mind, the memory of the past and the sustained claim on the future are inherently intertwined.

In the depths of Egypt, on the brink of cruel and wearying slavery, the *parsha* of *Vayechi* bears the seeds of a better future.

HEARING YOUR OWN VOICE

1. When Jacob sees his grandchildren, Efraim and Menashe, he asks their father, Joseph, "Who are these?" (Genesis 48:8). Yet Jacob had already been with them in Egypt for almost twenty years. What was Jacob really asking Joseph?
2. To what degree are our actions functions of our personal, present needs or of our considerations for the needs of the future generations?
3. What advice would you give to your children?
4. *Ayeka?* We are all descendants of Jacob. In what way are you fulfilling his blessing: his connection to the Promised Land?

Shabbat Lunch

Raising Children

In his final words, Jacob blesses his sons. He speaks to each of his children differently each child receives a unique message. For the first time in Jewish history, the line of inheritance, the acceptance of the mission first transmitted to Abraham, is bestowed upon each and all the sons.

Is there a Jewish approach to raising children? What characterizes Jewish parenting?

"Educate a child according to its way, even when he grows old he will not depart from it" (Proverbs 22:6). What does "its way" refer to? Are children born with a natural "way" of their own, or are children born with a *tabula rasa* (blank slate) and then nurtured or socialized into their behavioral patterns? In contemporary parlance, are we products of "nature" or "nurture"?

While never underestimating the influence of environment or experiences, the Talmud relates that a person is born with natural qualities and inclinations. A child's "way" begins at conception. This "way" is then expressed through character traits, for example, being artistic or musical, introverted or extroverted, cerebral or experiential, and so on. These traits serve as the raw material of the child and are, in and of themselves, value-free, reflecting neither "good" nor "bad" behavior.

Thus the first challenge for parents is to observe carefully their child's behavior and attempt to discern his or her natural tendencies. Their conclusions should become the basis for the parents' expectations of the child. Expectations stemming from the parents' own desires rather than from the child's innate qualities will inevitably yield distress and frustration for both parent and child. The Talmud (*Shabbat* 156a) relates that if a child is born with an "affinity for blood" (i.e., aggressive tendencies), it is incumbent upon the parents to perceive this quality and to direct it positively. If the parents are unsuccessful, the child may become a violent criminal; if the parents are moderately successful, the child may become a *shochet* (ritual slaughterer of animals), and if the parents direct this tendency productively, the child may become a *mohel* (circumciser).

Hence the primary role of parents is to help the child understand, fulfill, and productively channel his or her "way." For this reason, the Talmud (*Baba Batra* 21b) reports that only with great reluctance did the rabbis accept and introduce public elementary school education. Prior to this, home education allowed the parents to mold the educational process according to the unique traits of their child, to the child's being, the child's "way"; in contrast, formal group education focuses more on transmitting objective content and maintaining social discipline, frequently inhibiting the child's creative potential.

The ultimate test of the parents' success will be the child's direction of his or her natural qualities toward the common benefit, toward something beyond him- or herself, toward the improvement of the world. The self-awareness that the child develops will eventually yield an independent personality and maximize the child's potential contribution to society. Independent thinking does not simply manifest itself when the child has reached adulthood. Rather, its roots are present from the very first moments of a child's life, as the parents endeavor to understand that the child already possesses, and must strive to fulfill, its own "way."

The Midrash states that on his deathbed Jacob was worried that not all his sons would continue his struggle to establish monotheism in the world. When he asked them, they replied, *"Shema Yisrael* [Jacob's other name], the Lord is our God, the Lord is one." They affirmed Jacob's primary tenet of belief; each, in his own way, would be devoted to Jacob's mission.

HEARING YOUR OWN VOICE

1. *Pirkei Avot* (Ethics of the Fathers) 5:21 states that the decade of one's twenties should be dedicated to "pursuit" (dreams, exploration, etc.). How might this be connected to the discovery of one's own way?

2. Do you know any parents who, in your opinion, successfully raised their children each in his or her own "way?" What was the key to their success?

3. What do you think characterizes your "way"?

4. *Ayeka?* Your "way" includes strengths and weaknesses, gifts and shortcomings. Are some of these difficult for you to acknowledge? What advice would you give yourself to help you become more accepting of them?

Seuda Shlishit

Friendship beyond Words

Jacob blessed each of his sons with a different blessing. The tribe of Zebulun, for example, was destined to grow wealthy through trade and commerce. The tribe of Yissachar was gifted with intellectual skills, excelling in the learning of Torah. The Midrash (*Bamidbar Rabbah* 13:17) relates that together, these two brothers created an ideal friendship and partnership. Zebulun shared his financial wealth with Yissachar; Yissachar shared his wealth in learning with Zebulun.

The Hasidim tell the story of another ideal friendship:

The Rebbe of Vorke and the Rebbe of Trisk were childhood friends. They went to school together; they were inseparable. As time passed, they both became leaders of Hasidic dynasties.

They made a promise to each other that every week, they would write letters to each other. A Hasid was chosen and given the honor of delivering the letters between the rebbes.

Every Friday morning the Yorker Rebbe would hand an envelope to the Hasid, who would carry it through the woods till he reached Trisk and give it to the Trisker Rebbe. Usually within just a few minutes, the Trisker Rebbe would give him a letter in response, and he would carry it back to Yorke. Each time the rebbes would open the letter, huge smiles would appear on their faces.

This continued for week after week, year after year, for over fifteen years.

Then, one time, while the Hasid was carrying the letter to the Trisker Rebbe, a thought suddenly passed through his mind. "I have been carrying these letters for over fifteen years, and I have never once dared to open up the letters of the rebbes. I wonder what they are saying to each other?"

The thought nagged at him ceaselessly, until he could no longer control himself. With trembling fingers he opened the rebbe's letter. Inside was only a blank piece of paper. The Hasid was overcome with astonishment and confusion. "Can it be that for fifteen years I have been delivering blank letters?"

He delivered the letter to the Trisker Rebbe and received another one in return. As on his way to Trisk, he could no longer control himself. This time he tore open the envelope only to find – another blank piece of paper!

The Hasid delivered the letter to the Yorker Rebbe, but later on that night he was ridden with guilt and curiosity. He could not sleep.

Early the next morning he rushed to the rebbe, confessing. "Rebbe, I have to talk to you. After all these years, I couldn't resist. I opened your letter. But all I found was a blank piece of paper. Rebbe, I'm ashamed that I opened your letter, but Rebbe, please explain to me, have I been carrying blank letters for fifteen years?"

The rebbe comforted the Hasid with a kind look, and then began to explain. "You have to understand. The rebbe from Trisk and I have a very special relationship. A relationship that goes well beyond what words can express. Sometimes we do send actual letters to each other. But sometimes the letters are blank. You see, sometimes we don't have the words to express how we feel about each other. What we want to communicate can only be done on a blank piece of paper."

HEARING YOUR OWN VOICE

1. Why do you think the two rebbes made this agreement of sending weekly letters? Do you think that it was for the giver or the receiver of the letter?
2. Often partnerships, like that of Yissachar and Zebulun, develop into deep and lasting relationships. Why do you think this is so?

3. Did you *ever* send or receive a "blank letter?

4. *Ayeka?* What might one of your friends need from you? What gift could you give to one of your friends?

———————————————

Shemot

Slavery and Freedom

In the first five chapters of the book of *Shemot*, two themes are woven together: the beginning of the subjugation of the Jewish people and the emergence of Moses as their leader.

First, a new king (Pharaoh) reigns over Egypt, issuing decree after decree enslaving the nascent Jewish people and afflicting them with increasingly hard labor. Year after year, generation after generation, the Jewish people toil in servitude. Finally Pharaoh ordains that all their newborn sons shall be cast into the river. "And it came to pass in the course of those many days, that the king of Egypt died, and the children of Israel sighed from their bondage, and they cried out…" (Exodus 2:23). There are no signs of rebellion, no clandestine plotting. Denied of all control over their plight, they are left to lament and bewail their pitiful situation.

In the midst of this travail, their future leader, Moses, is born. Separated from his family at infancy, he grows up in the palace of Pharaoh. His reality is diametrically opposed to that of his people. He never works for Pharaoh's taskmasters, never dreads their cruel beatings. The Midrash states that Pharaoh would hug and kiss young Moses and place his crown upon the child's head. While the

Jewish people were being enslaved, their future leader was being adorned with Pharaoh's crown.

Why does the Torah weave together two utterly distinct and seemingly opposing themes – the slavery of the Jewish people versus the luxury of Moses?

Why couldn't a leader emerge from within the people? Why didn't a Jew who had endured the bitter suffering of slavery foment the rebellion? Why was it necessary that he who brings the Jewish people to freedom be raised apart from his people, on Pharaoh's lap?

One of the tragic effects of slavery is the incremental submission to and acceptance of its reality, until the slave cannot imagine a different existence. Imperceptibly, the slave begins to see him- or herself as a slave, incapable of imagining a different life. The slave's loss of control over his or her time and actions eventually leads to the loss of control over one's own persona. Almost involuntarily, the slave begins to believe that-"just as my condition is unchangeable, so too am I." When Moses spoke God's words of the hope of redemption to the Jewish people, they could not hear him, "because of the smallness of [their] spirit and [their] hard labor" (Exodus 6:9). The hardness of their labor eventually debilitated and enslaved not only their bodies but their spirit and their self-image as well.

Concomitant with this self-perception comes a similar attitude toward others. Burdened by the hopeless drudgery of their predicament, slaves cannot imagine that any other slave might have the power to transform or transcend circumstances. Their collective slavery diminishes their individual self-value and consequently affects how they view each other.

Individually and collectively, the oppressive reality of slavery crushes the dreams and yearnings of the people. The not-too-distant memories of their ancestors in the Promised Land, or of Joseph and his pivotal role in Egypt, are obliterated through the daily harshness of their labors. Pharaoh succeeds in his objective of disabling the Jewish people, weakening them in both body and spirit.

The future leader must be wholly detached from this inescapable dilemma. Moses grows up as the heir apparent to the leader of the most powerful country of his time. His whole childhood is directed toward taking responsibility for a people. Growing up in the palace of Pharaoh, Moses undergoes an apprenticeship to power. According to several commentaries, Moses' initial reluctance to accept God's mission for him to help emancipate the Jewish people does not stem from his lack of self-confidence but rather from his concern that, because he has not shared their experience of slavery, they will not listen to him.

These two themes – (1) a nation trying to sever its bonds of physical and psychological enslavement, and (2) Moses' attempt to assert his leadership and have it accepted by the people – will continue to be woven together throughout the entire book of Exodus.

HEARING YOUR OWN VOICE

1. Moses remonstrates with God that he cannot talk to the Jewish people because of the "heaviness" of his speech (Exodus 4:10). God then appoints his brother Aaron to be Moses' mouthpiece. Yet the entire book of Deuteronomy is a single speech of Moses. Why do you think that Moses thought that he could not speak to the people, and what happened to change that perception?

2. At the beginning of the Siddur (prayer book) is a blessing thanking God for not making one a slave. During the Holocaust, in the ghetto of Kovno, the question was asked if it was still appropriate to utter this blessing. The rabbi of Kovno responded that, then of all times, it was essential to recite it. Why do you think he gave that answer?

3. The redeeming leader, Moses, did not emerge from amid the people. The Talmud states, "A person cannot become a prophet

in his home city." Why? Do you think that friends and relatives promote or hinder a person from making changes in his or her life? Why?

4. *Ayeka?* We all become stuck in different times in our lives. Who in your life needs you to be "Moses" – to help them "unstick" themselves?

Shabbat Lunch

Having Children

The first chapter of *Shemot* describes the afflictions that Pharaoh decrees upon the Jewish people, culminating with "Every son that is born you shall cast into the river…" (Exodus 1:22). How do the Jewish people respond to their increasing hardship? There are no signs of rebellion or clandestine plotting, but are there any subtle indications that the Jewish people somehow defy their adversity?

The beginning of the account of the response of the Jews, the opening verse of the second chapter of this *parsha*, is remarkable only in its vagueness. "And a man from the house of Levi went and betrothed a woman from the tribe of Levi" (Exodus 2:1). This man and woman would subsequently give birth to Moses, "And the woman conceived, and bore a son." Yet the Torah would not reveal the names of these two figures until the sixth chapter of Exodus, five chapters later, when we learn that "Amram betrothed Yocheved… And she gave birth to Aaron and Moses…" (Exodus 6:20).

Why does the Torah present Moses' mother and father as nameless figures? Why did Amram decide to marry Yocheved precisely at this juncture in history? And most important, what does this event, the advent of the Jewish resistance to Pharaoh's decrees, signify?

From the juxtaposition of events in the Torah it is known that Yocheved had given birth to their first two children, Aaron and

Miriam, prior to this betrothal. If Yocheved and Amram already were husband and wife, why was there a need here for a second betrothal? The Talmud (*Sotah* 21a) explains that immediately after Pharaoh decreed that Jewish males must be cast into the river, Amram publicly announced that it was now futile to bring children into this world and set a precedent for the community by divorcing his wife. His daughter, Miriam, then castigated him, claiming that his decree was harsher than that of Pharaoh, since Pharaoh had only dictated that sons were to be thrown into the river, while Amram's decision included daughters as well. Persuaded by his daughter, Amram remarried his former wife, Yocheved. It is this betrothal that this week's *parsha* refers to. Thus the first defiance of Pharaoh's decrees was the decision to continue to have children.

Since Amram and Yocheved already have a son and a daughter, do they have any responsibility to have more children? What are the criteria by which to decide the number of children to have?

The Mishnah (*Yevamot* 61b) states that a man should not refrain from the mitzvah to "be fruitful and multiply" (Genesis 1:28) unless he has had two children. The Talmud then comments that the school of Shammai defined this parameter in terms of two males, based either upon the example of Moses (who had two sons, Gershom and Eliezer) or Adam (who had two sons, Cain and Abel). The ruling (*Shulchan Aruch, Even HaEzer* 1:5) eventually sided with the school of Hillel who posited that one has fulfilled the mitzvah to "be fruitful and multiply" by having one daughter and one son, based upon God's creation of the world with one male and one female, Adam and Eve.

The Talmud further states that a person who has had children in his youth should, nevertheless, continue to have children in his "old age." Maimonides writes that "even if one has fulfilled this mitzvah, one should not refrain from bearing children while he still has vigor, as any Jew who brings another being into this world has, in effect, built a whole world" (Laws of Marriage 15:16).

Amram and Yocheved were introduced anonymously, known

simply as "a man from the house of Levi … and a woman from the tribe of Levi" (Exodus 2:1). At this crossroads in history, their individual identities are not significant. Instead, the Torah are portrays them as the prototypes of a man and woman who chose, despite the inherent dangers, to continue to have children. Since they already have two children, their decision to remarry and have another child serves as an inspiration for the whole community. This act of courage and leadership resulted in the birth of Moses, the next leader of the Jewish people.

HEARING YOUR OWN VOICE

1. According to Jewish law, one only fulfills the mitzvah of "be fruitful and multiply" through having grandchildren. Why might this be so?

2. Yocheved and Amram chose to have another child, Moses, who eventually led the Jewish people out of their bondage in Egypt. The Talmud (*Shabbat* 119b) states that the verse, "Do not touch my anointed ones [messiahs]" (Psalms 105:15) refers to children who are studying Torah, and that the world only continues to exist because of their learning. Furthermore, it adds that one should not interrupt the learning of children even to rebuild the Temple and that any city that does not have a school for children should be either destroyed or excommunicated. Why do you think that the rabbis chose these ways to convey the centrality of the education of children? Do you think that this emphasis is reflected in your society today?

3. How many children would you like to have? Why?

4. *Ayeka?* Is there an act of defiance that you need to carry out in order to give future generations more hope?

Seuda Shlishit

Removing A Holocaust Number

This week's *parsha* describes the first persecution of the Jewish people. "And Pharaoh charged all his people, saying, 'Every son that is born you shall cast into the river …'" (Exodus 1:22). In the twentieth century, during the Holocaust, the Jewish people were once again forced to suffer from the decrees of an evil ruler. The memory of these tragic experiences did not vanish with the conclusion of the war. After the Holocaust, Rabbi Oshry, the former rabbi of the Kovno ghetto, wrote a book of responsa, including questions he was asked both during and after the Holocaust period. One such question dealt with removing numbers branded by the Germans on their Jewish victims. Rabbi Oshry writes:

> After the liberation, a young woman from a respected family asked me the following question. Since the Germans had branded her with a number in accord with their system of assigning numbers to every prisoner in the concentration camp, she wanted to have plastic surgery performed to remove the mark that constantly reminded her of the horror of those years. According to Jewish law, was it permissible to remove the number?

> RESPONSE:
> The Germans branded these numbers on the arms of Jews as a sign of shame, as though to say that the bearers of these branded numbers are not human beings but cattle to be brutally beaten, tortured, and slaughtered at will.

> Not only should these numbers not denigrate us but, on the contrary, such a number should be viewed as a sign of honor and glory, as a monument to the unforgivable bestiality of those

vile murderers. As part of the plot to exterminate the Jewish people ... the branded numbers guaranteed that if a Jew ever escaped from a camp, the imprint on his arm would reveal to everyone who found him that he was a Jew and fair game to be put to death.

The obligation to recall the entire scope of the Holocaust, not taking our minds off it for even a moment, is today a redoubled obligation, [to prevent] the world from forgetting the evils that the Germans perpetrated.

I feel that this woman should under no circumstances remove the branded number from her arm, for by doing so she is fulfilling the wishes of the German evildoers and abetting their effort to have the Holocaust forgotten, as if we Jews had created a fiction against them. Let her wear the sign with pride.

HEARING YOUR OWN VOICE

1. The memories of persecution and evil continue long after the events have passed. How do you think that the experience of slavery in Egypt continued to affect the Jewish people after their exodus? In what ways do you think the Holocaust continues to affect the Jewish people today?

2. What do you think is the purpose of remembering and commemorating tragedies that have befallen the Jewish people? Do you agree that there is an obligation to remember the Holocaust? Why?

3. Have you ever experienced anti-Semitism in your life? How did you respond? Does its memory still affect you?

4. *Ayeka?* What advice would you give yourself for wearing your Jewish identity with more pride?

Va'era

The Hardened Heart of Addiction

And the Lord said to Moses, ... "You will speak all that I have commanded you, and Aaron your brother will speak to Pharaoh, that he send the children of Israel from his land.... But Pharaoh will not listen to you, and I will place my hand on Egypt, and I will bring ... my people, the children of Israel, out from Egypt in great miracles." (Exodus 7:2–4)

And Pharaoh hardened his heart at this time also, and would not let the people go. (Exodus 8:28)

The *parsha* of *Va'era* describes the first seven of the ten plagues that afflict Egypt. With ascending vehemence, the supremely powerful people of Egypt is rendered utterly helpless, the most fertile of countries becomes a wasteland. Over the span of more than a year, the people of Egypt live in psychological terror of the visitation of the plagues. All this transpires because "Pharaoh will not listen to you."

During the first five plagues, despite Pharaoh's witnessing of the continual ravaging of his land, despite the warnings and their fulfillment, he refuses to accede to Moses' request to let the Jewish people go. (During the last five plagues, God "hardens" Pharaoh's heart, removing his free will.)

Why didn't Pharaoh listen to the warnings of Moses and Aaron? Why didn't Pharaoh change his mind? What does it mean, "to harden one's heart"? What prevented Pharaoh from seeing the folly of his decisions and led him to bring about the devastation of his own people and land?

Pharaoh imprisoned himself in a reality from which he could not escape. Despite the drastic consequences, Pharaoh was unable to change. He had become addicted. To what? To himself. He singlehandedly ruled Egypt, acquiring for himself the status of a god, neither respecting nor considering any contrary opinions. He rejected the advice of those closest to him (Exodus 10:7), and having convinced himself of his mythical powers and exaggerated position, he sought absolute control.

Paradoxically, in the end, Pharaoh loses all control – over his nation, his people, and even himself. The one who attempts to enslave an entire people, ironically, becomes the epitome of a slave, bereft of any power to alter his life. He becomes addicted to his set of principles, his vision of himself, his power. This addiction precludes any change. Despite the clear and disastrous consequences, Pharaoh refuses to adjust his convictions. How does this happen?

The Talmud (*Yoma* 87a) affirms that someone who says, "I will sin and [afterward] repent, I will sin and [afterward] repent," will not be able to actualize his repentance. Why not? The Talmud's repetition of the declaration implies that the declaration is not an isolated remark; rather, it represents a habit, a syndrome. The sinner continues to perform the same actions, while simultaneously thinking that it will be possible to change these actions or to disassociate from them. Eventually this dissonance will be resolved in favor of the action, as the habit will become part of the person's normative behavior. The Talmud contends that *the action will control the person more than the person will shape the action*. Despite the expressed desire to abandon the behavior, eventually we will somehow rationalize our actions and convince ourselves that the actions were justified.

Pharaoh, having convinced himself for so long that he possessed complete and supreme control over his nation, fell victim to his own self-perception. He could not listen to others and eventually imprisoned himself in his own conceptions. His worldview became petrified, his heart became hardened, and he himself became a slave.

HEARING YOUR OWN VOICE

1. The quintessential conflict in Egypt is reflected in the personalities of the respective leaders, Moses and Pharaoh. In what way is Moses the antithesis of Pharaoh? Who do you think is a more typical prototype of leadership?

2. Why do you think that some people are more able to listen than others? At what times are you more ready to listen and change your mind than at others? Why?

3. How is it possible to "soften" someone's hardened heart?

4. *Ayeka?* Everyone has "buttons" or triggers that evoke knee-jerk reactions. What is one of your "buttons"? What step could you take to help you engage your heart, soul and brain before reacting automatically?

Shabbat Lunch

Getting Closer

And God spoke to Moses, and said to him, "I am the Lord; and I appeared to Abraham, to Isaac, and to Jacob by the name of God Almighty [El Shaddai], but my name, the Lord [Ado-nai], I did not make known to them." (Exodus 6:2–3)

The beginning of this week's *parsha* involves a breakthrough in the relationship between God and Moses. Though there have already been numerous prophetic revelations in the Torah in which God's words are communicated to the patriarchs and matriarchs, nevertheless, the beginning of this *parsha* manifests a qualitatively new and deeper stage in the relationship between God and humanity. A new name of *God – Ado-nai –* is revealed.

The revelation of this name indicates that Moses achieves a closeness with God that eludes all the previous figures in the Torah. The mystics considered the name *Ado-nai* to be the most intimate and holy name of God. Whereas other names of God may express qualities of power, mercy, or creation, this name is comprised of the past, present, and future constructs of the verb "to be" in Hebrew, indicating God's eternality and transcendence.

Why did God disclose this special name only to Moses? Furthermore, why did this breakthrough occur precisely at this moment in their relationship?

There is one fundamental change that transforms God's relationship with Moses: the emergence of the Jewish people. Moses has now become the spokesman for the Jewish people, not only to Pharaoh but also to God. He does not speak to God from the vantage point of an individual Jew but rather as the representative of an entire people. At the end of last week's *parsha*, after Pharaoh refused to allow the Jewish people to leave Egypt and increased the intensity of their labors, Moses challenged the effectiveness of God's actions. "And Moses returned to the Lord and said, 'Lord, why have you dealt badly with this *people* ... You have not saved Your *people* at all'" (Exodus 5:22–23). God does not reveal this new name to Moses – the individual prophet – but rather to Moses, the spiritual/political leader of his people.

Moses speaks not as an individual but rather as a representative of the Jewish people. It is on this national level that God now relates to him and thus enables their relationship to reach more profound depths. All the previous figures in the Torah had related to God either as individuals or as forerunners of a future people. For each of them, the existence of the Jewish people possessed a dreamlike quality, a hope or an abstract vision. For Moses, however, the vision becomes reality. This aspect of the relationship, the impending destiny of the Jewish people, becomes the focus between God and Moses and several verses later will culminate with "And I will take you to me for a people" (Exodus 6:7).

This model of the growth and deepening of a relationship between God and Moses is also applicable to the human realm. While two individuals may develop a serious attachment to each other, if it is limited to the scope of their particular worlds and personalities, part of their beings will never be shared, names will not be disclosed. The sharing of dreams, goals, or concerns that are beyond personal well-being will afford insight and understanding into each other that their purely personal, individual bonds would most likely not generate. In Moses' case, God revealed a new name, reflecting a new level in their relationship.

When Rabbi Akiva, one of the most romantic personalities of the Talmud, proposed to his wife, he promised her a bracelet engraved with "Jerusalem of Gold." Their love for each other transcended their individual personalities and bonded them with the Jewish people and Jerusalem.

HEARING YOUR OWN VOICE

1. Moses achieved a deeper relationship with God because he represented the Jewish community. One of the rationales for the requirement of a minyan for prayer is to indicate that each Jew needs a community to fulfill his spiritual self. Why is it preferable to develop one's spiritual self in the context of a community? Do you think that there is a potential danger in developing one's spiritual self alone?

2. In the blessing after eating, *Birkat Hamazon*, additional names of God are inserted if there are more than ten men. An opinion in the Mishnah (*Berakhot* 7:3) suggests inserting additional names of God if one hundred, one thousand, or ten thousand men are present. Were you ever in a setting of thousands or tens of thousands of Jews? Did this affect your Jewish identity or your relationship with God? In what ways? Why?

3. Did you ever experience a moment in which you were functioning not only as an individual but also as a representative of the Jewish people?

4. *Ayeka?* What advice would you give yourself to help you better connect and contribute to the Jewish People?

Seuda Shlishit

Courage and a Modern Pharaoh

> And the Lord spoke to Moses, saying, "Go in, speak to Pharaoh, king of Egypt, that he may let the children of Israel go out of his land." (Exodus 6:10–11)

Moses' courageous example of confronting Pharaoh and demanding freedom for the Jewish people has been replicated countless times in Jewish history. Natan Sharansky resolutely defied the totalitarian regime of the Soviet Union and campaigned for the right of Soviet Jews to emigrate to Israel. For his beliefs, he was sentenced to thirteen years' imprisonment, including long stretches of solitary confinement. Following is his statement to his accusers prior to his verdict:

> Five years ago I applied for an exit visa to emigrate from the USSR to Israel. Today I am further than ever from my goal. This would seem to be a cause for regret, but that is not the case. These five years were the best of my life. I am happy that I have been able to live them honestly and at peace with my conscience. I have said only what I believed, and have not violated my conscience even when my life was in danger.
>
> I feel part of a marvelous historical process – the process of the national revival of Soviet Jewry and its return to the homeland, to Israel. I hope that the false and absurd but terribly serious charges made today against me – and the entire Jewish people – will not impede the process of the national revival of the Jews of Russia, as the KGB has assured me they would, but will actually provide a new impulse, as has often happened in our history.
>
> My relatives and friends know how strong was my desire to join my wife in Israel.... For two thousand years the Jewish people, my people, have been dispersed all over the world and seemingly deprived of any hope of returning. But still, each year Jews have stubbornly, and apparently without reason, said to each other, *Leshana haba'a b'Yerushalayim* (Next year in Jerusalem)! And today, when I am further than ever from my dream, from my people, and from my Avital, and when many difficult years of prisons and camps lie ahead of me, I say to my wife and to my people, *Leshana haba'a b'Yerushalayim*. (*Fear No Evil*, p. 224)

Almost ten years later, Natan Sharansky saw the fulfillment of these words, as he was reunited with his wife, Avital, and his people, in Jerusalem.

HEARING YOUR OWN VOICE

1. It is stated in the Ethics of the Fathers (Mishnah, *Pirkei Avot* 4:1) that a "hero" is one who controls his or her own desires. Why do you think that the rabbis thought of heroism as a private, internal process?
2. Who is the most courageous person you know? Why?
3. Which Jewish value would you most adamantly defend?
4. *Ayeka?* What small step could you take to help you listen to the "Moses" voice within you – to become more of a leader?

Bo

A Battle of Futures

This week's *parsha*, *Bo*, culminates with the final three plagues. With intensifying frenzy, Egypt is plunged into darkness. First, hordes of locusts swarm like a black cloud over the land, then the plague of darkness grows successively more palpable, and finally, in the middle of the night, death strikes the firstborn. The yearlong drama of plagues has brought about the collapse and ultimate demise of Egypt. The Jewish people are on the verge of their exodus to freedom.

Why was the plague of the firstborn, the most ghastly of them all, chosen to be the decisive and culminating plague? Nine other plagues had attacked the land and animals of Egypt; now the angel of death was unleashed upon the Egyptian people themselves. But why did this angel of death strike only at the *children* of Egypt?! The adults of Egypt had enslaved the Jewish people; were they not responsible? Why were the adults not killed? Why, instead, were their children punished?

The *parsha* alternates between two themes: the present exodus and its future commemoration. At the very beginning of the *parsha*, God tells Moses, "Go to Pharaoh, for I have hardened his heart, and the heart of his servants, that I might show them My signs before him; and that you may tell in the ears of your children, and your child's children, what things I have done in Egypt..." (Exodus 10:2).

The celebration of Passover is detailed not only for the present generation that is about to observe it but also for all future generations:

> And this day will be a memorial for you ... throughout your generations you will keep it a feast by ordinance, forever. (Exodus 12:14)

> And you will observe this thing for an ordinance to you and to your children, forever. (Exodus 12:24)

Why does this *parsha* continually juxtapose the future observance of the children and grandchildren of the Jewish people with the impending plague that will strike the sons of the Egyptian people? Until this tenth plague, the conflict of the Jewish people in Egypt existed primarily between the two peoples and their respective leaders. At this juncture, the focus of the conflict shifts from the present to future. The plagues no longer destroy the *land* of Egypt and its inhabitants; now the thrust of the tenth plague is the destruction of the *future* of Egypt, its children. Pharaoh had ordered that the sons of the Jewish people be thrown into the Nile, hoping to obliterate their future; now, with Divine justice, the screams in Egypt announce that *its* future has been destroyed.

Passover celebrates the birth of the Jewish people. The Passover Seder centers on the children of each Jewish home. When a Jewish child is born, a song of joy is sung, "*Siman tov u'mazel tov* (it is a good sign and good luck) *y'heh lanu, u'l'chal Yisrael* (for us and for all of the Jewish people)." The birth of a child is the cause for both individual and collective rejoicing. As in this week's *parsha*, individual and collective futures are seamlessly interwoven.

HEARING YOUR OWN VOICE

1. The rabbis of the *Zohar* ask, "It is written, 'And it came to pass that at *midnight* the Lord smote all of the firstborn in the land of Egypt' (Exodus 12:29), but it is also written, 'And it came to pass on the *middle of that day* that the Lord did bring the children of Israel out of the land of Egypt …' (Exodus 12:51). Why did the Jewish people wait till the middle of the day, and not leave at night after the striking of the firstborn?" The *Zohar* answers that the Jewish people waited in order to create the stark contrast of one people going to freedom while the other people was burying its dead. For what other reasons might the Jewish people have waited for the middle of the day to leave?

2. On Passover we are supposed to simulate the exodus of the Jewish people from Egypt. What do you think that the Jewish people were thinking and/or feeling as they left Egypt?

3. Can a moment of epic proportions ever truly be remembered accurately? What are the inherent difficulties in eternalizing an experience? Are there any moments in your life that you have struggled to perpetuate?

4. *Ayeka*? The story of the Exodus has given hope to the Jewish People during its darkest hours. How do you give hope to others?

Shabbat Lunch

When Enemies Fall

Pharaoh, the greatest enemy the Jewish people had ever known, has been defeated. "And Pharaoh rose up in the night, he, and all his servants, and all of Egypt; and there was a great cry in Egypt;

for there was not a house where there was not one dead. And he called for Moses and Aaron by night, and said, 'Rise up, and leave my people, both you and your children of Israel, and go, serve the Lord, as you have said'" (Exodus 12:30–31).

How should the Jewish people respond to the downfall of Pharaoh and his people? How should they look upon the decimation of the very forces that tortured and enslaved them? Egypt had been their home for several generations. It had provided the food for their survival during the great famine in Israel. It had also reduced them to pathetic beings, bereft of spiritual, emotional, or intellectual vitality. Should they now rejoice? Or should they pity the Egyptians?

In next week's *parsha*, *Beshallach*, after the Egyptians drown in the sea, the Jews rejoice and sing, "I will sing to the Lord, for He has triumphed gloriously; the horse and his rider He has thrown into the sea" (Exodus 15:1). In his commentary on the verse, "when the wicked perish there is jubilation" (Proverbs 11:10), the Vilna Gaon writes, "When God takes revenge on their [the Jewish people's] enemies, then there is jubilation, as during [the drowning of the Egyptians] in the sea and as in Purim." These sources and historical realities indicate that the removal of dangers to the Jewish people and the destruction of evil is grounds for jubilation. An absence of rejoicing may reflect an inadequate grasp of the peril and oppression that the Jewish people underwent during these times.

A different approach is expressed in the Mishnah: "Samuel, 'the small one' [*hakatan*] would say: 'When your enemy falls, do not rejoice, and his stumbling should not gladden your heart, for the Lord may see it and find displeasure in it and He will remove His wrath from him'" (Ethics of the Fathers 4:24). Here, one is instructed not to rejoice.

This rabbinic figure, Samuel, was referred to as "the small one" because of his modest and unassuming nature. The Talmud notes several occasions on which he chose to accept public humiliation rather than have someone else suffer embarrassment. Nevertheless, one incident in his life, during the times of Roman persecution shortly after the destruction of the Second Temple, seems at first glance to be quite out of character. The leader of the Jewish people, Rabban Gamliel of Yavne, requested that the rabbis compose a prayer asking for the breakdown and eradication of the enemy forces that sought to destroy the Jewish people, both physically and spiritually. None of the rabbis complied until Samuel, "the small one," the one who had instructed that one should not rejoice when your enemy falls, stood up and singlehandedly created the prayer calling for the destruction of the enemies of Israel!

Many commentators understand that, in fact, only Samuel *bakatan* possessed the moral stature to pen this prayer. Only a person whose self-nullification would preclude the seeking of personal gratification over the downfall of his enemy could objectively pursue the eradication of evil. Only a person who had demonstrated that he sought no individual satisfaction could ask for the dissolution of the opponents of the Jewish people.

The resolution of the seeming contradiction between these two sources, "when the wicked perish there is jubilation" and "when your enemies fall, do not rejoice," may be resolved in a similar manner. One is instructed not to rejoice in the case of "*your* enemies." If one is personally involved and regards the adversaries as his or her own, then this subjectivity may impede an impartial understanding of the situation and we are cautioned against this potentially vindictive, retaliatory rejoicing. However, if one is able to remain objective, to realize that these enemies are not personal ones but rather adversaries of the entire Jewish people, then his or her rejoicing reflects communal joy of enabling the Jewish people to advance and flourish.

HEARING YOUR OWN VOICE

1. The Talmud relates that whenever there was a drought, the rabbis would go to Abba Chilkiya and urge him to pray for rain.

One time, upon being asked, he went up to his roof and prayed in one corner while his wife prayed in the other corner. The rain clouds gathered over her corner. Abba Chilkiya remarked that this was because of her exceptional merit. One time there were some troublemakers in his neighborhood and Abba Chilkiya prayed that they should die, while his wife prayed that they would reform their ways (*Taanit* 23b). With whom do you naturally identify more – Abba Chilkiya or his wife?

2. Do you know anyone who reminds you of Samuel *hakatan*?
3. Did you ever defeat an adversary? How did you feel afterward?
4. *Ayeka?* What advice would you give to someone who was planning to retaliate personally in revenge for acts committed against the Jewish people?

Seuda Shlishit

On Meeting a King

This week's *parsha* describes the culmination of the confrontation between Moses and Pharaoh, the king of Egypt. Shmuel Yosef (Shai) Agnon (1888–1970) was one of the central figures in Hebrew literature in the twentieth century. His works deal with the philosophical and psychological problems of his generation and include novels, folktales, and stories. On December 10, 1966, Agnon, upon receiving the Nobel Prize for Literature, also met with a non-Jewish king, the king of Sweden. The following is an excerpt from his acceptance speech.

Your Majesty, Your Royal Highnesses, Your Excellencies, Members of the Swedish Academy, Ladies and Gentlemen:

Our Sages of blessed memory have said that we must not enjoy any pleasure in this world without reciting a blessing. If we eat any food, or drink any beverage, we must recite a blessing over them before and after. If we breathe the scent of goodly grass, the fragrance of spices, the aroma of goodly fruits, we pronounce a blessing over the pleasure. The same applies to the pleasures of sight: when we see … the trees first bursting into blossom in the spring, or any fine, sturdy and beautiful trees, we pronounce a blessing. And the same applies to the pleasures of the ear.

It is through you, dear sirs, that one of the blessings concerned with hearing has come my way.

It happened when the Swedish Charge d'Affaires came and brought me the tidings that the Swedish Academy had bestowed the Nobel Prize upon me. Then I recited in full the blessing that is enjoined upon one who hears good tidings for himself or others…. And now that I have come so far, I will recite one blessing more, as enjoined upon he who beholds a monarch: "Blessed are You, Lord, our God, King of the Universe, Who has given of Your glory to a king of flesh and blood."

HEARING YOUR OWN VOICE

1. Why do you think that a special blessing was created to say upon seeing a king? What effect do you think that the hearing of this blessing might have upon a king?

2. Rav Kook, the first chief rabbi of Israel, wrote that a president or prime minister elected democratically acquires the status of a king, and should be honored accordingly. Is there anyone to whom you would afford this level of honor today?

3. Have you ever, upon meeting someone for the first time, been inspired to recite a blessing or other words commemorating the event? Who inspired such a reaction?

4. *Ayeka?* What comes to mind as your most noble or dignified act? Looking back, what does this act evoke within you now?

Beshallach

Friday Night Meal

Growing Pains

The *parsha Beshallach* bridges the two historic events of the book of Exodus: the departure of the Jewish people from Egypt and their experience at Mount Sinai. Within the span of seven weeks, the Jewish people will metamorphose from an enslaved mass of individuals to a united people embracing holiness and divine purpose. *Beshallach* recounts their journey out of Egypt into the wilderness of the desert, their fears, their joys, and the travails of their nascent independence.

The journey out of Egypt climaxes with the miraculous parting of the sea, which saves the Jewish people from the advancing Egyptian army. The Jews spontaneously respond with a poetic explosion of song, replete with musical instruments and dancing. Yet seemingly only moments after celebrating their supernatural deliverance, the Jewish people begin to bemoan their pitiful state, complaining about the bitterness of the available water. This complaint is followed by further murmuring over the lack of food and then once again over the lack of water. Only days removed from their house of bondage, the Jewish people have already began to wax nostalgic for their preferable conditions in Egypt: "Would that we had died by the hand of the Lord in the land of Egypt, when we sat by the flesh pots, and when we ate our fill of bread..." (Exodus 16:3).

How could the Jewish people have become so ungrateful? How could they complain about mundane realities such as food and water in light of their miraculous experiences? How could a people who had endured the slavery of Egypt and who would soon stand at Mount Sinai rapidly become so preoccupied and distressed over food and water?

The journey from Egypt to the Promised Land was much more than a trek across the desert. It was a period of transformation and maturation of a people who had assumed a slave mentality.

The Torah describes the journey of the Jews through the desert as follows: "And the Lord went before them by day in a pillar of a cloud, to lead them the way; and by night in a pillar of fire to give them light; that they might go by day and night" (Exodus 13:21). They traveled according to divine guidance. Their nourishment was supplied for them without their laboring: "And the Lord spoke to Moses saying, 'At evening you shall eat meat, and in the morning you shall be filled with bread' (Exodus 16:11–12) ... and the children of Israel ate the manna for forty years, until they came to inhabited land" (Exodus 16:35). Even their wars were fought miraculously. "And it came to pass, that when Moses held up his hand, Israel prevailed; and when he let down his hand, Amalek [the enemy] prevailed" (Exodus 17:11). The Midrash adds that not only did their garments never wear out during their forty years in the desert, but that they even expanded with them so that no one ever lacked for clothing.

What visual image of the Jewish people is being created through all these dimensions of their life in the desert? A nation of children, a nation undergoing the childhood of its development. What characterizes childhood? While traveling or walking, children hold their parents' hands (symbolized by God's nocturnal fire and daily cloud). In the eyes of children, food is never lacking; it miraculously and effortlessly appears, like the manna in the desert. In times of conflict, parents providentially arrive to rescue their children from any peril, as God rescued the Jews in their victory over Amalek. Even their clothes, from the vantage point of young children, are purchased and cleaned by an invisible source.

The exodus from Egypt represents the birth of the Jewish people. It marks the beginning of the childhood of their national existence. Subsequently, the stage of adolescence will be reflected through their struggle with the prophets' instructions during the First Temple period (approximately 996–586 BCE). Adulthood will be simulated during the Second Temple period (516–70 CE), epitomized by the hiddenness of God and the emergence of rabbinic authority. Seen in this historical perspective, the limited scope and brazen impatience of the Jewish people at this time, while perhaps disappointing, may be construed as natural growing pains in the long journey to adulthood.

HEARING YOUR OWN VOICE

1. In the *parsha* of *Beshallach*, the Jewish people are given a new mitzvah. In the midst of their complaining, they are told to collect manna for six days but to refrain from collecting it on Shabbat. Instead they should prepare a double portion of food on the sixth day, because on Shabbat no manna will fall. One of the messages of Shabbat is patience – that whatever work consumes us during the week can wait. Why is this an appropriate lesson for the Jewish people at this stage of their development? What else do you think that the idea of *Shabbat* might convey to them?

2. The two momentous events of the last two *parshiyot* (portions), the exodus from Egypt and the splitting of the sea, impart

different messages. Of the two, the exodus is considered to be the essential moment, whereas the splitting of the sea has been referred to by commentators as "God's superfluous miracle, the miracle that comes to reflect God's love for the Jewish people." Why?

3. What qualities of childhood, adolescence, or adulthood do you see in the Jewish people today?

4. *Ayeka?* At every age, we still have the voice of the child within us. When have you recently listened to your child voice? What do you love about your child's voice? What advice would you give to yourself to help you tune in to your adult voice?

Shabbat Lunch

Overcoming Fear

The Jewish people leave Egypt and after six days reach the unbridgeable sea. The Egyptian soldiers and chariots are pounding on their heels. They cannot return to Egypt, nor can they advance, as the sea is in front of them. "And Egypt pursued after them, all the horses and chariots of Pharaoh, and his horsemen, and his army, and overtook them encamping by the sea ... and the children of Israel lifted up their eyes, and behold, Egypt marched after them; and they were very much afraid" (Exodus 14:9–10). Panic rages throughout the camp. Frenzied questions abound. The people attack Moses, "... have you taken us out to die in the wilderness? Why did you do this to us, to take us out of Egypt?" (Exodus 14:11).

How will the Jewish people overcome their fear? How does anyone overcome fear?

Moses' attempt to allay the fears of the Jews is rejected by God. "And Moses said to the people, 'Fear not, stand still, and see the salvation of the Lord, which He will show you today ... the Lord will fight for you, and you will hold your peace" (Exodus 14:13–14). The Talmud (*Sotah* 36b) states that Moses' plea to the people infuriated God: "'My beloved people are on the verge of drowning in the sea, and you are spinning out lengthy prayers before Me?!' Moses said to God, 'But what else can I do?' God replied, 'Speak to the children of Israel that they go forward!'"

The same section of the Talmud describes the pandemonium besieging the camp. Rabbi Yehuda said, "One tribe said, 'I will not be the first to go into the sea'; and another tribe also said, 'I will not be the first to go into the sea.' While they were standing there deliberating, Nachshon ben Aminadav sprang forward and jumped into the sea. As he entered it, the sea parted." Nachshon's courage and willingness to walk into the unparted sea saved the Jewish people.

How did Nachshon have the courage to jump in?

Rabbi Eliyahu Dessler, a leading rabbi of England and Israel in the twentieth century, offers an insight into how one can strive to overcome feelings of anxiety. He writes that one of the underlying psychological causes of worry is often a sense of guilt, a subconscious feeling that one actually deserves punishment. A person's inner notion of unworthiness, of fault, or of insecurity over his or her actions may result in the incessant agonizing over the consequences of his or her decisions. One feels that one is simply not worthy of receiving benevolence. Thus, writes Rabbi Dessler, the focus of one's concern, one's fear, should always be focused on improving oneself, on improving one's self-image and fulfilling one's moral potential. All moments of fear are likely to be external manifestations of this problem of lack of self-esteem.

Through his feat Nachshon became an eternal symbol of courageous action for the Jewish people: he transcended fear and worry and generated positive results. The Talmud states that, following his example, future leaders of Israel would continually emerge from Judah, his tribe.

HEARING YOUR OWN VOICE

1. Why did God delay the parting of the sea? What was achieved by causing such stress to the Jewish people? Apparently God did not want to fight for the Jewish people while they waited passively. The Jewish people needed to learn how to transcend their worries and fear, how to move beyond their present trauma, and especially, they had to learn not to rely exclusively on God to perform miracles for them. Do you think that one can learn to transcend fear and worry?

2. The Ba'al Shem Tov, the founder of Hasidism, once said that life is like climbing a ladder. If one wants to climb to the next rung in life, one must be willing to endure a moment of instability, when only one foot is on the ladder and the other is in the air, between the rungs. Have you ever experienced this feeling? How did you cope with the period of uncertainty?

3. Have you ever felt paralyzed by worry or fear? Why? Do you know any people who seldom worry? Why do you think they seem so calm?

4. *Ayeka?* What is one small and practical step you could take to feel more worthy of God's benevolence?

Seuda Shlishit

Poet Parachutist

While the Jewish people trembled with fear, waiting for the sea to part, Nachshon ben Aminadav bravely dove in to the sea (see *"Beshallach:* Overcoming Fear"). Nachshon's courageous act established a historic precedent of being daring and taking risks to ensure Jewish survival. Over three thousand years later, a young woman would follow in his path and became a modern symbol of hope and heroism.

Hannah Senesh, born in 1921 in Budapest, Hungary, settled on a kibbutz in Israel in 1939. At an early age she revealed exceptional intellectual and literary talent. In 1943, Hannah joined thirty-one volunteers in a dangerous rescue mission. Their plan was to para-chute into enemy territory and attempt to liberate Allied pilots who had been shot down behind Nazi lines. After completing their mission, they intended to make contact with underground partisan fighters and to rescue Jews trapped in Romania, Hungary, and Czechoslovakia. Hannah parachuted on March 13, 1944. After completing the first stage of her task, she was captured by the Hungarian police and brutally interrogated for months.

A well-known poet, Hannah wrote several poems while in her prison cell, including:

> One-two-three ... eight feet long,
> Two strides across, the rest is dark ... Life hangs over me like
>   a question mark.

> One-two-three ... maybe another week,
> Or next month may still find me here, But death, I feel, is
>   very near.

> I could have been
>   twenty-three next July;
> I gambled on what mattered most,
> The dice were cast. I lost.

Days before her execution she pressed a small piece of paper into the hand of another member of her mission. It contained the poem that would become known by heart by virtually every Israeli school child.

> Blessed is the match consumed in kindling flame.
> Blessed is the flame that burns

in the secret fastness of the heart.

Blessed is the heart with strength to stop its beating for
  honor's sake.

Blessed is the match consumed in kindling flame.

Shortly after her period of interrogation, Hannah Senesh was executed by a Nazi firing squad. She is buried at the Israeli military cemetery of Mount Herzl in Jerusalem.

HEARING YOUR OWN VOICE

1. What do you think that Hannah Senesh was trying to express in her poem "Blessed Is the Match"?

2. Hannah Senesh's act of bravery was not an isolated moment in her life; rather, it reflected her entire approach and passion for life. At the age of seventeen she wrote in her diary, "One needs something to believe in, something for which one can have wholehearted enthusiasm. One needs to feel that one's life has meaning, that one is needed in this world." What is this "something" for you?

3. What is the most courageous or giving act that you have ever witnessed? That you have ever done?

4. *Ayeka?* What is holding you back from being braver?

Yitro

Wonder and Mystery

Fifty days after their exodus from Egypt, the Jewish people stood at Mount Sinai, ready to receive the Ten Commandments. For Moses, this moment represents the return to the spot where God had originally chosen him to lead the Jews out of slavery. The diminutive burning bush has now become a mountain, where the course of human history would, in a single moment, be indelibly changed. God's promise to Moses at the beginning of this book has been fulfilled; Moses' mission has been completed: "And God said to Moses, 'I will be with you ... in your bringing the people out of Egypt to serve God *on this mountain*'" (Exodus 3:12).

Yet the minute after the Jewish people depart from Mount Sinai, it reverts to being merely another mountain in the howling wilderness of the desert. The exact location of Mount Sinai is not known. It does not acquire eternal sanctity; eternal words were spoken at a *transitory site*.

In this week's *parsha*, however, the words of the Ten Commandments (Exodus 20:1–14) seem to be very much dependent upon the events occurring at Mount Sinai. The preceding chapter

134

(Exodus 19) struggles to find the words and images to describe the setting of Mount Sinai. "And it came to pass on the third day in the morning, that there were *voices* [thunder?] and lightning, and a thick cloud upon the mountain, and the voice of a shofar was *exceedingly strong*, and all the people in the camp trembled . . . and Mount Sinai was enveloped in smoke . . . and the *whole mountain trembled* . . . and the voice of the shofar became *stronger and stronger*" (Exodus 19:16–18). After the Ten Commandments are given, the Torah states "the people *saw the voices* [!] and the fires and the voice of the shofar and the mountain of smoke and the people saw it and were shaken and stood at a distance" (Exodus 20:15).

What is this otherworldly description attempting to convey? Could the content of the Ten Commandments have been given without the dramatic setting of voices, lightning, and blasting of the shofar?

When the Jewish people arrived at Mount Sinai, they knew very little about themselves. Most likely they were aware of their ancestors, their patriarchs and matriarchs. They knew that they were different from the Egyptians and that they were headed toward the Promised Land. But what did they know of their collective identity or responsibility? Did they have any idea how they would begin to fulfill the prophecy to Abraham of "being a blessing" and that "through him [them] all the families of the world would be blessed?" Their collective identity remained unknown.

The relationship between God and the Jewish people is created through both articulate and inexpressible domains. The Ten Commandments represent the revelation of the *content* of this relationship. Beyond the "letter of the law" of this relationship, however, lies an infinite dimension of the relationship that can never be communicated through speech. The description of the events at Sinai before the giving of the Ten Commandments struggles to convey that which is beyond conveying, that which is beyond all sensory reception, the indescribable, the mysterious. The images of the primal sound of a shofar becoming louder and louder, the "seeing" of the voices, a mountain trembling on fire, all strive to transmit a sense of wonder and awe.

In chapter 19, before the Jewish people receive the Ten Commandments, they are told that their collective destiny is to become a "nation of priests, a holy people." To achieve this goal, they must acquire a sense of living for "something beyond" their material reality. The Midrash states that the Torah is "black fire written on white fire." The black fire is represented by the letters, the white fire by the spaces between the letters, that which could not be limited to words. There is much more white fire than black fire. This moment of grandeur and mystery then becomes the foundation for the collective Jewish attempt to see the sublime in all of existence.

Abraham Joshua Heschel writes:

> Awareness of the divine begins with wonder. It is the result of what man does with his higher incomprehension. The surest way to suppress our ability to understand the meaning of God and the importance of worship is to take things for granted. Wonder or radical amazement is the chief characteristic of the religious man's attitude toward history and nature. The profound and perpetual awareness of the wonder of being has become a part of the religious consciousness of the Jew. (*God in Search of Man,* p. 46)

Mount Sinai was a moment in history. This moment has continued to reverberate through time, throughout the universe. The establishment of the national Jewish identity begins with a sense of wonder.

HEARING YOUR OWN VOICE

1. In the song that we sing at the Pesach Seder, "*Dayenu,*" it says that "if God had brought us near to Mount Sinai and had not

given us the *Torah – dayenu* (it would have been enough)." How could one understand this?

2. What moments have engendered a sense of wonder and/or awe in your life? Do you know people whose lives are generally filled with a greater sense of wonder? Why do you think that this is so?

3. How might the idea of "white fire and black fire" shed light on human relationships? What is the potential hazard of only seeing the black fire or only the white fire?

4. *Ayeka?* Have you ever had a spiritual moment? What do you think you could do to be more open to having spiritual moments?

Shabbat Lunch

Studying Torah – "Means" or "End"?

This week's *parsha, Yitro,* records the giving of Torah at Mount Sinai. For countless generations, the Jewish people have bonded together through the learning of Torah. Throughout history, and most recently during the Holocaust, Jews risked their lives to learn Torah.

What is the purpose of this learning? Is the learning of Torah an "end" in and of itself, or is it the "means" to achieve a further goal?

Approximately two hundred years ago, Rabbi Chaim of Volozhin, the foremost student of the Vilna Gaon, wrote his epic work *Nefesh HaChaim.* There he states that the goal of studying Torah is the learning of Torah itself. "The truthful understanding is that one should learn Torah 'for its own sake'" (section 4, chapter 3). No other ulterior motive should be involved. Rabbi Chaim further explains that studying Torah is tantamount to coming closer to God, and through learning Torah a countless number of mystical worlds are created and redeemed. While learning Torah, one is allowed to break for several minutes daily to strive to purify one's thoughts and to strengthen one's fear of Heaven, but the primary focus of one's studies should be exclusively the learning at hand. This represents the highest endeavor possible for humanity.

A different approach was adopted by the Maharal of Prague, almost four hundred years ago. In his sermon on Rosh Hashanah, the Maharal decried the deplorable quality of learning in his community. Although the members of his community faithfully spent their time learning, the Maharal lamented that their approach to the learning of Torah was flawed. He wrote that their love of learning Torah was so strong that it had eclipsed the purpose of their learning, namely, to bond with the Giver of Torah, God. The learning of Torah is the path through which one is able to receive and express one's love for God. His community's love for learning had, ironically, become an obstacle in their relationship with the transcendent. The studying of Torah should serve as the "means" through which one advances one's relationship with God.

A third approach is reflected in a discussion that took place almost two thousand years ago. The Talmud (*Kiddushin* 40b) relates that the rabbis raised the question, "Which is greater – learning or doing?" Rabbi Tarfon asserted that practice is more important, while Rabbi Akiva advocated learning. The rabbis deliberated on these responses for a period of time and finally concluded enigmatically "learning is greater, because it brings one to action." From their answer, it is not clear whether the rabbis sided with Rabbi Akiva or Rabbi Tarfon, because while they stated that learning is "greater," they emphasized it as a means to an end – action. Later commentators clarify that the intention of the rabbis was not to endorse either of the two perspectives, but to establish a comprehensive approach to the learning of Torah. The process of learning Torah, when performed correctly, should necessarily result in action. According to this approach, one's behavior should stem from the learning of Torah, and, conversely, the true purpose of learning Torah is to affect one's course of action.

HEARING YOUR OWN VOICE

1. In his book *Nefesh HaChaim*, Rabbi Chaim points out a number of dangers when the study of Torah is understood as a "means" and not as an "end." Can you think of any? Can you think of any dangers when it is understood as an "end?"
2. With which of these three approaches – learning for its own sake, learning to bond with God, or learning to affect one's actions – do you most agree? What argument could you make for the other two points of view?
3. In the blessing recited before the learning of Torah, we ask that our learning always be sweet. Have you ever had any moments of learning that you would consider to have been "sweet?"
4. *Ayeka?* What do you think holds you back from being impacted by your learning? What could you do to be more affected by what you learn?

Seuda Shlishit

Learning in Danger

The value of learning Torah has been essential to the Jewish people since their inception. The Talmud (*Berakhot* 61b) recounts a famous parable depicting the centrality of this learning.

> One time the evil rulers decreed that the Jewish people were prohibited from engaging in the learning of Torah. Papus ben

Yehuda found Rabbi Akiva publicly convening large groups of people to study Torah.

He said to him, "Akiva, aren't you afraid of the rulers?"

He replied, "I will tell you a parable. What is our situation comparable to? To a fox that was walking by the side of the river, and saw fish scurrying from place to place. The fox asked them, 'Why are you fleeing?' They told him, 'We are escaping from the nets of the fishermen.' He said to the fish, 'Would you like to come up to the dry land, and we will live together, just like our ancestors lived together?' They replied, 'Are you the one that they say is the most clever of the animals?! You are not smart at all. If, in the place that gives us life [water] we are afraid, all the more so will we be afraid in the place of our death [dry land].'"

Continued Rabbi Akiva, "So too it is with us. Now that we are engaging in the learning of Torah, which is our sustenance, and our situation is so dire, if we desist from this learning, all the more so will our situation deteriorate."

It was said that not many days passed until Rabbi Akiva was caught and imprisoned. The rulers also placed Papus ben Yehuda in jail with him. Rabbi Akiva said to him, "Papus, what brings you to this place?" He replied, "Fortunate are you, Rabbi Akiva, that they arrested you on account of your learning Torah; woe to Papus, who was caught because of petty offenses."

HEARING YOUR OWN VOICE

1. Why are the images of fish and water used as symbols of the Jewish people and Torah?
2. During the Holocaust the question was often asked, "Is one obligated to endanger one's life to try and continue learning Torah?" The rabbis ruled that one was not required to risk one's life in order to learn. Does this judgment contradict the example set by Rabbi Akiva?

3. Do you know of anyone who has gone to considerable lengths or sacrifice to further his or her learning of Torah?
4. *Ayeka?* What step could you take to increase the quantity or quality of your learning?

Mishpatim

Enslaving Love

What could possibly have followed the moment of sublime inspiration of voices, lightning, and shofar at Mount Sinai?

Seemingly anticlimactic, the *parsha* of *Mishpatim* begins abruptly with a list of over fifty new laws, ranging from various degrees of murder and stealing to accidental damages and negligence. Still standing at Mount Sinai, the Jewish people no longer are "seeing the voices and the lightning" (Exodus 20:15). The sound of the shofar reverberates only in their memories. Now their lives and reality are about to be transformed through this-worldly laws and judgments. Almost one hundred verses will elaborate the particular rules that will govern their nascent society.

What could the Jewish people have been thinking during this lengthy enumeration of regulations? Until this time, most of the laws that they had received had dealt with the Passover sacrifice and the departure from Egypt. A moment earlier, they had encountered the Ten Commandments, general in content and inspiring in message. But this list is much different. The details of their marketplace and community, the basic fabric of their daily lives, must

142

now reflect this Sinai experience. No longer the slaves of Pharaoh, the Jewish people cannot for a moment refrain from their mission of becoming a "nation of priests and a holy people" (Exodus 19:6).

Is there an order to the listing of laws in *Mishpatim*? Does the arrangement of the laws reflect subtle priorities? Rav Kook wrote that just as there are laws in poetry, so too there exists poetry in laws. What message is underlying the sequence and system of these laws?

The laws in this *parsha* progress in descending order of severity. Intentional manslaughter is followed by accidental homicide, then kidnapping, then injuring another. Then come the laws of reparations when a person's animals or indirect actions kill or harm another. Eventually one is held responsible for neglecting to return a lost object to one's enemy (Exodus 23:4) and even for helping one's enemy to unload his or her animal. In this progression from the most severe transgression to the lesser ones, what stands out in bewildering fashion is the placement of the first law of this list: the buying and keeping of a Jewish servant (slave). Apparently, there is a quality or situation concerning the Jewish servant that, in the eyes of the Torah, supersedes even manslaughter!

The system of slavery in Judaism, no longer practiced, was actually a form of social rehabilitation. The Torah does not mention the institution of prisons. Incarceration was not considered to be a viable solution. The Torah does not regard a criminal as a deviant but as one in need of help. It is the responsibility of the community to assist the criminal to alter his or her behavioral patterns. The goal is not to remove the criminal from society but rather to enable him or her to return and productively contribute to society. To achieve this goal, a criminal was "adopted" by a family for six years, hopefully to learn from its example how to better conduct his or her life, and then be "let free," to return to society as a completely independent member.

The family that chose to "adopt" this criminal assumed the position of "foster parents" and was responsible for educating and helping the servant amend erring habits. The family members were obligated to call a servant by his or her name and not employ derogatory labels. If this servant had a profession in his or her former life, the family was not allowed to demand work in a different field. The family was required to maintain the servant's honor; the Midrash proscribes requesting that the servant do any menial or self-degrading acts (Leviticus 25:43). Throughout the Torah (the *parshiyot* of *Behar*, Leviticus 25, and *Re'eh*, Deuteronomy 15) this servant is continually referred to as "your brother."

The Talmud explains that the case of slavery in this week's *parsha* is of a man who had not managed his finances correctly, had ended up irretrievably in debt, and consequently had been apprenticed to another family. This process should ideally give him a second chance to learn how to successfully manage his income and return to society. It is hoped that he will mature and learn to live with greater foresight, so that ultimately he will be able to accept full responsibility for his actions.

The chance of tragic failure of this system is reflected in the beginning of this week's *parsha*. What happens if, after six years of "second childhood," the servant chooses to remain a servant? "And if the servant will continually say, 'I love my master, my wife, and my children; I will not go out free,' then his master shall bring him ... to the doorposts [*mezuzot*], and his master shall bore his ear through with an awl; and he will serve him forever" (Exodus 21:5–7).

The servant chose to remain a servant, "a slave." The first of the Ten Commandments states "I am the Lord your God Who brought you out ... of the house of bondage" (Exodus 20:2). Now this servant says, "I love my master," which is a denial of freedom, a denial of the lesson of the exodus. In response, the servant is brought to the doorposts of the house. In Egypt, the Jews placed the blood of the *paschal* sacrifice on the doorposts of their homes, symbolizing their freedom from human masters, from Pharaoh. The servant has his ear branded with an awl at this doorpost. "Rabbi Yochanon Ben Zakkai said, 'Why was the ear singled out from all of the other bodily parts?' Said God: 'The ear which heard my voice on Mount Sinai when I said, "that the Jewish people are my servant unto me," and then went and acquired for himself another master, let it be branded"' (*Kiddushin* 22b).

Apparently in the eyes of this week's *parsha*, even more serious than the physical damages that one may inflict upon another is the crime that one can do to oneself: the rejection of freedom, the denial of independence, the choosing to remain a slave.

HEARING YOUR OWN VOICE

1. Why might the "slave" have chosen to remain a slave? What do you imagine that the slave thought as he was being led to the doorpost?

2. After this period of adoption, this "second childhood," the servant chose to remain a child. The servant's adopting family did not inculcate in the servant a desire for freedom and independence. What do you think the mistake of the family might have been?

3. What advice would you suggest today for someone afraid to face the freedom and adversity of adulthood?

4. *Ayeka?* What idea, attitude, or habit enslaves you today?

Shabbat Lunch

Overcoming Hatred

On occasion, the Torah presents two verses that appear to be remarkably similar, yet upon a closer reading, significant differences emerge. Two such verses, one in this week's *parsha* and one in *Ki Tetze* (Deuteronomy 22:4), seem to invite examination and comparison.

> If one sees a donkey of one that hates you (or you hate him) collapsing under its burden, and you consider resisting to assist him, then you must surely assist him. (Exodus 23:5)

> You should not see the donkey or ox of your brother fall and ignore them [the donkey and ox], you should surely raise them up with him. (Deuteronomy 22:4)

Though the examples are similar, as both involve the distress of someone else's animals, there are at least two clear differences. In the first case (Exodus), the relationship with the owner of the animal is one of hatred, whereas in the second case (Deuteronomy) it is one of closeness. Second, the situation of the two animals is not identical. In Exodus, the animal has been overburdened and is presently suffering under this load; in Deuteronomy, commentators explain that the verse refers to the owner's belongings, which were on the animal and have fallen, and now the owner is in need of help to load the animal again. The case in Exodus emphasizes the suffering of the animal, while that in Deuteronomy accents the misfortune of the owner of the animal.

The Talmud (*Bava Metzia* 32b) raises a third hypothetical situation and poses the following question: "If one were to encounter two situations at exactly the same time: (1) someone he *hated*, who needed assistance in *loading* his animal, and (2) someone he *liked* whose animal needed to be *unloaded* from its burden – who should one help first?"

At first glance, the question may seem simple, since one is required to remove unnecessary pain from animals, and only the animal who is overburdened is in need of immediate help. Nevertheless, the Talmud answers, "It is a mitzvah to help the one he hates first, in order to curb his desire [of hatred]!" Although a person's natural inclination might be to help the animal in distress and to assist his or her friend, the first priority in the eyes of the Talmud is to restrain and emend his or her current feelings of hatred. The power of hatred may eventually intensify and become uncontrollable. Slowly it grows to be virulent and destructive and may ultimately become self-consuming, affecting not only the particular relationship involved but also influencing all of a person's actions and general frame of mind. The effort to reduce this hatred supersedes other rightful concerns, even the suffering of an animal.

How does the act of assisting an enemy reduce the enmity between the two people?

The act of working together shifts the focus of the two parties from the tension between them to their shared objective of loading the animal. The Talmud adopts the principle that a person's emotions are influenced by his or her actions. The act of kindness, even when performed in the context of an unfriendly relationship, impels the doer to lessen feelings of anger, to "curb his desire." Then, once one of the parties involved has changed the status quo and created a positive environment, a window of potential reconciliation has been opened.

The Book of Knowledge (*Sefer HaChinuch*), written anonymously in the eleventh century, generalizes this principle into an all-embracing approach to human relationships. "More than a person's thoughts direct his actions, one's deeds ultimately shape one's heart." A person's behavior will eventually greatly influence his or her emotional composition.

In an antagonistic relationship, it is precisely the witnessing of the misfortune of a hated person, that may afford an opportunity to overcome hatred, for one's own sake as well as for the sake of the relationship.

HEARING YOUR OWN VOICE

1. The Torah and Talmud propose a number of methods for sublimating and overcoming hatred, but they never instruct a person to eradicate the power to hate. Why might this be so? Could there be a worthy dimension to the capacity to hate?

2. Have you ever felt such hatred or anger that it influenced your

other relationships or impeded your functioning? How did you resolve it?

3. Has your emotional state ever been shaped by your actions? How so?

4. *Ayeka?* What advice would you give yourself to become a more compassionate human being?

Seuda Shlishit

A Corrected Judgment

This week's *parsha* lists many of the laws that the judges of the Jewish people are required to enforce. Yet judgments are not only made by legal authorities and do not occur exclusively in courts of law. Every day, individuals form opinions and evaluate the actions and attitudes of those around them. The following is a story of mistaken judgment related by Rabbi Shlomo Carlebach.

An orphan had been taken captive and was being ransomed for five thousand rubles. The townspeople did not have enough money to pay the ransom, so they turned to the rabbi of the town, Rabbi Shneur Zalman, the founder of Chabad Hasidism. When the townspeople came to Rabbi Shneur Zalman, he was sitting with two other rabbis, Rabbi Menachem Mendel of Vitebsk and Rabbi Levi Yitzchak from Berditchev. After hearing the townspeople, he told them not to worry, he would ask "Moishele the miser" for money. The two rabbis were shocked. "Don't you know that Moishele hasn't given money to anyone in twenty years!"

"Do not worry," replied Rabbi Shneur Zalman.

The three rabbis went to see Moishele the miser. Rabbi Shneur Zalman knocked on his door. Moishele was surprised to see the three rabbis. He allowed them to enter and the three rabbis sat down.

Rabbi Shneur Zalman began to explain the grave situation of the child, how they needed to pay the ransom of five thousand rubles. Moishele listened intently and then said, "I am sorry but I cannot help you." Rabbi Shneur Zalman accepted Moishele's words, stood up, and gave Moishele a blessing. The three rabbis prepared to leave, but as they were closing the outside gate, Moishele opened the door to the house and ran after them, calling out, "Wait, wait. Come back. I have changed my mind." The rabbis returned to the front door.

"Rabbi, I have changed my mind." Moishele opened his hand and gave Rabbi Shneur Zalman one kopeck (one penny). It was an old and dirty kopeck. But Rabbi Shneur Zalman put his hand over Moishele's and thanked him effusively for his gift. The two other rabbis remained silent, baffled by the depth of appreciation shown by Rabbi Shneur Zalman.

As the rabbis were leaving for a second time, Moishele again summoned them back, calling out, "Wait, wait. Come back. I have changed my mind." Again the rabbis returned, and again Moishele gave Rabbi Shneur Zalman one kopeck.

Again and again, the rabbis would leave and Moishele would call them back. First it was another dirty kopeck, then a new one. Soon he began to give five kopecks, then ten, then five rubles, then ten rubles, then one hundred, then five hundred, until Moishele had given Rabbi Shneur Zalman all five thousand rubles. Each time he gave something, Rabbi Shneur Zalman would thank him profusely for his gift.

Later that night, the two rabbis turned to Rabbi Shneur Zalman and asked him if he knew all along that Moishele would give them the five thousand rubles so desperately needed. Rabbi Shneur Zalman replied, "Do you remember anything special about the first kopeck that Moishele gave us?"

"Yes, it was old and dirty, almost black."

"Yes," answered Rabbi Shneur Zalman. "You see, Moishele had the potential to become one of the most generous people, but someone had to be willing to take that first kopeck. Every time that someone asked him for money, he would open his hand and show them the old and dirty kopeck, and no one would take it from him. That was all that he was able to give at that moment, but everyone expected him to give more. No one let him give what he was able to at that moment. I saw that if I just accepted what he was able to give then, that would gradually open him up and enable him to give more. And so it was."

HEARING YOUR OWN VOICE

1. What do you think that Moishele was thinking or feeling when he gave that first "dirty kopeck"?
2. The previous story is a paradigm for all human interaction. Can you think of other (nonfinancial) examples of miserliness and, according to this model, how they might be overcome?
3. Have you ever had the wisdom and perception to accept "a dirty kopeck" from someone, somehow knowing that that was all they could give at that time? How did you know? Did someone ever accept "a dirty kopeck" from you?
4. *Ayeka?* What do you think you could do to become less judgmental?

Terumah

The Unknowable

The *parshiyot* (portions) of the Torah often come in pairs, the second *parsha* expanding and deepening themes introduced in the first. The two *parshiyot* dealing with the laws given at Mount Sinai, *Yitro* and *Mishpatim*, are now succeeded by two *parshiyot* detailing the construction of the Tabernacle (in Hebrew, *Mishkan*, dwelling place), *Terumah* and *Tetzaveh*. *Terumah* primarily elucidates the building of the *Mishkan* and its components, while *Tetzaveh* describes the clothes and consecration of the priests who worked in the *Mishkan*.

The *Mishkan* structure, approximately twenty meters long, was located at the center of the Jewish encampment. It was divided into two rooms. The larger room, referred to as the "Holy Chamber," housed the menorah, the table, and the golden altar; the smaller room, known as the "Holy of Holies," housed the ark that contained the tablets of the Ten Commandments. The daily work of the priests (*kohanim*) occurred in the larger room, while the "Holy of Holies" was restricted solely to the service of the High Priest (*Kohen HaGadol*) once a year, on Yom Kippur.

151

Though the idea of the *Mishkan* seems very far removed from today's reality, in the world of the Torah it represents the completion of a process that has extended for over a book and a half (Genesis and half the book of Exodus) and lasts twenty-six generations. In paradise, the Garden of Eden, humanity could hear the voice of God. Since the loss of paradise, however, the spiritual harmony between God and humanity had been broken. Finally, at Mount Sinai, this relationship is restored. Heaven and earth touch. But the Jewish people cannot remain at Mount Sinai forever.

What would eventually happen to this Sinai experience with the passing of time? Would it simply vanish once the Jewish people began to journey, fading with the weakening of its memory? How could the Jewish people preserve this life-changing, world-changing moment?

The ultimate purpose of the *Mishkan* was to create a physical space that would sustain the spiritual bond between God and the Jewish people, which reached a peak at Mount Sinai. "And there I [God] will meet with you, and I will speak with you from above the covering [of the ark]" (Exodus 25:22). Nachmanides, a medieval Torah commentator, refers to the *Mishkan* as a portable Mount Sinai. Every relationship requires renewing, rekindling, and, sometimes, repairing. The *Mishkan* was the vehicle that served these purposes for the relationship between God and the Jewish people.

The symbolism of the structure and components of the *Mishkan* convey the secret to preserving the relationship between God and the Jewish people. This week's *parsha* details the two principal utensils in the "holy chamber," the table and the menorah. The table, located on the northern side of the *Mishkan*, held twelve breads that were eaten by the priests working in the *Mishkan*. The breads symbolized the physical and material nourishing of the Jewish people. The Talmud (*Bava Batra* 25b) writes that one who wanted to prosper financially should look at the table and draw inspiration from it.

The menorah, a seven-branch candelabrum lit daily by the *kohanim*, was located on the southern side of the *Mishkan*. Its light symbolized human enlightenment and understanding. The Talmud relates that one who wanted to become wise would look at the menorah (*Bava Batra* 25b). Similarly, the women of Tekoa (village south of Jerusalem) were known to have been wise because of their meticulous use of olive oil in lighting their Shabbat candles (*Menachot* 85b). These sources gave birth to the customs on Friday night of gazing at the Shabbat candles after lighting them and during the making of Kiddush.

The holy chamber, exemplifying the material and intellectual achievements of humanity, was not, however, the final destination. It was the antechamber, the room that led to the essence of the *Mishkan*, the "Holy of Holies" (*Kodesh HaKodashim*). Therein rested the ark that held the tablets of the Ten Commandments, the physical reminder of humanity's connection to the transcendent.

Yet this chamber, the heart of the *Mishkan* and the Jewish camp, was off limits to virtually all the Jewish people. More than anything else, the "Holy of Holies" symbolized that which was unapproachable, inaccessible, beyond the human domain. Unlike today's synagogues, which are intended to be places of gathering and prayer, the *Mishkan* was primarily the house of mystery.

The presence of this unapproachable, unknowable reality, this hidden room, would preserve the memory of the moment of Mount Sinai. The primary obstacle to sustaining the spiritual harmony between humanity and God is the lack of awareness that there is something beyond this physical world. The failure to hear God's voice is often simply a result of not listening. The hiddenness of the "Holy of Holies" continually reminded the Jewish people of the "unknowable" reality in this world, inviting them to listen and be influenced by that which lies beyond.

HEARING YOUR OWN VOICE

1. Do you think that simply looking at the table or the menorah could actually change someone's behavior? Why?
2. If you were to construct your own *Mishkan*, what would you put into the "Holy of Holies"?
3. In your own life, what places or moments, experiences or coincidences, have made you more aware of "the unknowable?"
4. *Ayeka?* When was the last time you felt you were having a holy moment?

Shabbat Lunch

Tzedakah – Giving or Taking?

The Jewish people are about to create their first national sanctuary, the *Mishkan*. Where will the resources come from? "And the Lord spoke to Moses, saying, 'Speak to the children of Israel that they bring a contribution for Me; every person according to the generosity of his heart will bring something'" (Exodus 25:1–2). Only months ago, the lives of the Jews had been drastically overturned, and they had left Egypt with only their most portable possessions. Now they were being asked to willingly donate some of their belongings for the building of their sanctuary. Will they give enough? "And all the wise men that carried out all the work of the sanctuary ... spoke to Moses saying, 'the people bring much more than enough for the task' ... and Moses commanded and proclaimed throughout the camp, saying, 'Let neither man nor woman do any more work of contributing to the building of the sanctuary.' So the people were restrained from bringing" (Exodus 36:4–6). Thus the people responded overwhelmingly with "the generosity of their hearts."

But what would have happened if the Jewish people had been less amenable to Moses' request, if their hearts had been reluctant to contribute to the building of the sanctuary? Would Moses have compelled them to donate to the collective cause? Should one be forced to give *tzedakah* (charity)?

Almost one thousand years ago, Maimonides wrote: "We have never seen or heard of a Jewish community that does not have a *tzedakah* fund.... We must observe the precept of *tzedakah* more carefully than any other positive commandment.... No one ever becomes poor from giving *tzedakah*" (Laws of Gifts for the Poor, chapters 9–10).

Maimonides also delineated guidelines for giving, clarifying eight degrees of charity, each one higher than the other:

> FIRST LEVEL: The giver enables the recipient to become self-supporting.
>
> SECOND LEVEL: Neither the giver nor the recipient is aware of the other's identity.
>
> THIRD LEVEL: The giver knows the recipient, but the recipient does not know the giver.
>
> FOURTH LEVEL: The recipient knows the giver, but the giver does not know the recipient.
>
> FIFTH LEVEL: The giver gives directly to the recipient without being solicited.
>
> SIXTH LEVEL: The giver gives directly to the recipient after being solicited.
>
> SEVENTH LEVEL: The giver gives less than she or he should, but cheerfully.
>
> EIGHTH LEVEL: The giver gives begrudgingly.

The highest degree (first level) is to aid a Jew in need by offering him a gift or loan, by entering into a partnership with him, or by providing work for him, so that he may become self-supporting, without having to ask people for anything.

What is special about the "second level" of giving, being unaware of the other's identity, making it superior to the remaining levels?

Maimonides refers to this level, which has the highest degree of anonymity, as "doing a mitzvah for its own sake." Rabbi Eliyahu Dessler writes that every act can be classified as either an act of "giving" or of "receiving." Either the person is motivated to act for the sake of a greater cause, independent of personal reward and satisfaction ("giving"), or else she or he is driven by a personal need of self-gratification ("taking"). Similarly, each particular act can have varying degrees of the qualities of "giving" and "taking."

When an individual gives *tzedakah,* how does he or she truly know whether this is a purely giving act or if it is mixed with certain elements of self-gratification? According to the eight levels of Maimonides, when the giver does not require personal accolades or even a moment of recognition, then he or she knows that the money has been given for the sake of giving, of "doing a mitzvah for its own sake." Though a person has fulfilled the mitzvah of *tzedakah* if he or she has given according to any of these eight levels, nevertheless, this highest stage represents an ideal. Furthermore, this act of sincere giving should then become a paradigm for all of one's behavior in the future.

HEARING YOUR OWN VOICE

1. According to Jewish law, it is preferable to give small amounts many times than to give a single large amount. Why should this be so?
2. Why do you think that Judaism turned *tzedakah* into a commandment that a person must do regardless of how he or she feels at the present moment and does not leave the decision of giving to the impulses of one's heart?
3. What act of *tzedakah* stands out most in your mind? By others? By yourself?

4. *Ayeka?* What do you think you could do to give with a more open heart?

Seuda Shlishit

Fund-Raising

Since their very inception, the Jewish people have been noted for their giving *tzedakah.* In January of 1948, Golda Meir was sent on a crucial fundraising mission for the soon-to-be declared Jewish state. She writes in her autobiography:

> We were, of course, totally unprepared for war. That we had managed for so long to hold the local Arabs at bay, more or less, didn't mean that we could cope with regular armies. We needed weapons urgently, if we could find anyone willing to sell them to us; but before we could buy anything, we needed money – millions of dollars. And there was only one group of people in the whole world that we had any chance of getting these dollars from: the Jews of America. There was simply nowhere else to go and no one else to go to.
>
> Who would go? At one of these [governmental] meetings, I looked around the table at my colleagues, so tired and harassed, and wondered for the first time whether I ought not to volunteer for the mission. After all, I had done some fund-raising in the States before, and I spoke English fluently.... I began to feel that I should suggest this to Ben-Gurion. At first, he wouldn't hear of it.... "Then let's put it to a vote," I said. He looked at me for a second, then nodded. The vote was in favor of my going.
>
> "But at once," Ben-Gurion said. "Don't even try to get back to Jerusalem." So I flew to the States that day – without any luggage, wearing the dress I had worn to the meeting with a winter coat over it.

The first appearance I made in 1948 before American Jewry was unscheduled, unrehearsed and, of course, unannounced.... I didn't speak for long, but I said everything that was in my heart. I described the situation, as it had been the day I left Palestine, and then I said:

"The Jewish community in Palestine is going to fight to the very end. If we have arms to fight with, we will fight with them. If not, we will fight with stones in our hands.... My friends, we are at war. There is no Jew in Palestine who does not believe that finally we will be victorious. That is the spirit of the country ... but this valiant spirit alone cannot face rifles and machine guns.

"You cannot decide whether we should fight or not. We will. The Jewish community in Palestine will raise no white flag for the mufti. That decision is taken; nobody can change it. You can only decide one thing: whether we shall be victorious in this fight or whether the mufti will be victorious. That decision American Jews can make. It has to be made quickly, within hours, within days. And I beg of you – don't be too late. Don't be bitterly sorry three months from now for what you failed to do today. The time is now."

They listened, and they wept, and they pledged money in amounts that no community had ever given before.... By the time I came back to Palestine in March I had raised $50,000,000, which was turned over at once for the Haganah's secret purchase of arms in Europe.... Ben-Gurion said to me, "Someday when history will be written, it will be said that there was a Jewish woman who got the money which made the state possible." But I always knew that these dollars were given not to me, but to Israel. (*My Life*, pp. 213–214)

HEARING YOUR OWN VOICE

1. The Talmud (*Bava Batra* 9a) states in the name of Rabbi Elazar that one who causes others to give *tzedakah* has greater merit

than those who actually give the *tzedakah*. Why do you think that this is so?

2. What would you have said if you had been in Golda Meir's place? Have you ever been in the position of asking others to contribute to a cause? Were you successful?

3. What cause(s) do you most believe in supporting?

4. *Ayeka?* What holds you back from giving more generously?

Tetzaveh

Clothes of Humility

This week's *parsha* concludes the two *parshiyot* (portions) that describe the building of the Tabernacle and the sacred service. The first *parsha, Terumah,* describes the external nature and physical construction of the Tabernacle. The second, *Tetzaveh,* concentrates on human responsibility within the Tabernacle and focuses on the primary caretakers of the Tabernacle: the *kohanim* (priests). *Tetzaveh* begins with the daily lighting of the menorah by the *kohanim* and concludes with their offering of the daily sacrifice and burning of the incense. From the beginning of the book of Exodus until the conclusion of the Torah, this will be the only *parsha* in which the name Moses does not occur, focusing exclusively upon the role of Aaron, his brother, and Aaron's descendants, the *kohanim.*

The book of Genesis relates that Jacob had twelve sons, each of whom became the founder of his respective tribe. Each tribe ultimately had its own location within Israel, its own special attributes, and its own particular responsibilities to perform for the sake of the Jewish people. The tribe of Levi, Jacob's third son, was eventually divided into two groups: the *kohanim,* who were responsible for

160

the service of the Tabernacle, and the Levites, who assisted them in their duties. *Tetzaveh* recounts the consecrating of the *kohanim*. "And you [Moses] should select Aaron and his sons from out of the Jewish people to administer to Me...." (Exodus 28:1) "And Aaron and his sons I will sanctify to minister to Me in the Priest's capacity" (Exodus 29:44).

From birth, the *kohanim* were different from the other tribes. They were trained for holiness. Their whole lives were dedicated to the performance of their holy work in the Tabernacle in the desert and, ultimately, in the Temple in Jerusalem. Particular laws and practices separated them from all of the other tribes of Israel. They did not own land or engage in practical trades. They were allowed to eat specially ordained foods that possessed higher spiritual qualities (tithes). To this day, *kohanim* are limited in whom they are permitted to marry and are not allowed to come into contact with dead bodies. The Talmud states that the *kohanim* were both God's spiritual messengers to the Jewish people and the Jewish people's spiritual messengers to God (*Yoma* 19a).

In light of all this, the thrust of *Tetzaveh* is surprising. The major concern of this week's *parsha* is the specification of the special clothes that the *kohanim* were obligated to wear while working in the Tabernacle. Almost fifty verses, half of the whole *parsha*, describe the garments of the priests in great detail. None of the other tribes were obligated to wear particular clothes. Moreover, the work of the *kohen* was utterly dependent upon his wearing these clothes; a *kohen* performing holy service in the Tabernacle without any piece of his clothes was subject to the death penalty.

Why were the *kohanim* singled out to wear a special uniform? Were they simply clothes of identification?

Doesn't the emphasis on these external symbols contradict the spiritual, internal thrust of the *kohanim*'s lives? The more elevated and spiritual the role of the *kohen*, the greater the emphasis the Torah placed on his clothes – four for the other priests and eight for the High Priest. Why?

One effect of wearing the priestly clothes cited by the Talmud (*Zevachim* 88b) is that each particular garment possessed special atoning qualities that influenced the behavior of its wearer. For example, the special pants worn by the priests atoned for sexual promiscuity and the tiny ringing bells at the bottom of the coat reminded the wearer not to speak gossip.

The Talmud relates that the continual work in the Tabernacle and the Temple transformed the nature of the *kohanim*. They became the most zealous tribe, purified in thought, meticulous in detail. Their role utterly separated them from the rest of the Jewish people and perpetually reminded them of their special stature and holy occupation. And, perhaps, therein lay the single greatest danger to the successful functioning of the Tabernacle-the danger of the *kohanim*'s gradual feelings of spiritual superiority, of self-righteous conceit. Will their automatic hereditary status engender a vain pompousness, an elitist disdain for those whose lives do not center around the Holy of Holies?

The clothes of the *kohanim* were the primary vehicle that served to keep them humble. The clothes were contributed by the people of Israel and did not become the private possessions of their wearers. The wearing of these clothes was limited to the service of the Tabernacle; the Talmud states that the *kohanim* were not allowed to sleep in these special clothes and questions whether they were even allowed to walk in them while not involved in the actual services. Without these clothes, the *kohanim* could not take part in any of the holy ceremonies; only after donning the clothes that were bestowed upon them by the rest of the Jewish people were the *kohanim* able to function.

How can the Jewish people raise a select group dedicated to a life of holiness yet prevent them from becoming a holy aristocracy? By perpetually reminding them that they are indebted to all those whom they are presently serving, that their privileged function is solely a result of the contributions of all the Jewish people. Every time the *kohanim* prepared themselves for their work, they had to dress themselves in the gifts from their people. They were continually reminded that not only do they represent the entire people but, as was told to the entire Jewish people at Mount Sinai, the whole nation is also, in fact, a *memlechet kohanim*, a nation of priests (Exodus 19:6).

HEARING YOUR OWN VOICE

1. What do you think are the positive and negative messages of clothes today? Does the example of the clothes of the *kohanim* have any relevance for contemporary society?
2. How might one raise children to a life of holiness today?
3. What safeguards would you suggest today to prevent self-righteousness among spiritual leaders?
4. *Ayeka?* What message do your clothes convey?

Shabbat Lunch

Worn-Out Clothes and Empty Synagogues

This week's *parsha, Tetzaveh,* focuses on the significance and centrality of the clothes of the *kohanim.* These clothes were essential to the *kohen's* role of caring for all matters of holiness in the Temple and even acquired a level of sanctity of their own. The Torah states that these clothes were to be holy garments, "for honor and for beauty" (Exodus 28:2), and Maimonides writes that because of their special stature, the clothes of the *kohanim* would always have to appear clean and new. They were never to be bleached or washed. Eventually, like all clothes, they would wear out. What would happen to them then?

What happens to an object of sanctity after it has fulfilled its purpose? Is it simply discarded or is its memory somehow sustained and hallowed? Is it still held in regard for the service that it once performed, or is it deemed dispensable?

The Talmud (*Sukkah* 41a) states that the *kohanim* would remove the hems of their worn-out pants and belts and then use them for wicks to light torches to illuminate the courtyard of the Temple during the celebrations of Sukkot, known as *Simchat Beit HaShoevah*. During the seven days of Sukkot, it was customary in Jerusalem to rejoice in communal singing and dancing. Though the clothes were no longer fit to be worn by the *kohanim*, they were not simply abandoned; they were appropriated to perform an additional function within the domain of the Temple-to light the holiday torches.

Other tasks may be found for the worn-out clothes of the *kohanim*, but what happens to a synagogue that is no longer needed by its community? Can a building that was once dedicated to the spiritual lives of its constituents, that housed sacred articles and books, now be sold? Can it be used for commercial or secular purposes? Among the many opinions mentioned in the Talmud, the rabbis stated that a synagogue may be sold with the stipulation that the new owners not turn it into a bathhouse, a tannery, a *mikveh*, or a laundry. These four possibilities all involve a more physical and less sacred level than the synagogue's former status.

The Mishnah further states in the name of Rabbi Yehuda that a synagogue that has been destroyed cannot be used for any other purpose; one may not even walk through it as a shortcut. If weeds grow inside it, they should not be pulled out, in order to intensify the anguish of those who see them. He explicates the verse "And I [God] have made desolate your holy places" (Leviticus 26:31) as meaning that "they are still holy places, despite having become desolate."

HEARING YOUR OWN VOICE

1. The Talmud (*Berakhot* 8b) relates that while in the desert, the Jewish people carried the shards of the first set of the Ten Commandment tablets with them for all forty years. Though broken, the original sanctity of the tablets merited their safeguarding. From this example, the Talmud learns that one should continue to give respect to an elderly person even after he or she has forgotten his or her learning. To what other examples would this principle apply?

2. Have you ever seen a synagogue now in disuse or being occupied for other purposes? How did it make you feel?

3. Do you have any possessions that you would not discard even after they have served their purpose? Why?

4. *Ayeka?* If you were to discard one piece of clothing that no longer reflects you, what would it be?

Seuda Shlishit

The Rabbi's Boots

Rav Chaim Soloveitchek (1853–1918), known as the "Brisker Rav," was one of the premier rabbinical figures of his time. Possessing outstanding analytical powers, he created a new approach to the study of Talmud, "the Brisker system," whose categories and terminology would influence the next century of Talmudic study. He was one of the leading rabbis and teachers of the famous Volozhin Yeshiva.

This week's *parsha, Tetzaveh*, describes the many clothes of the priests and High Priest. The priests, known for their eagerness and zeal, always performed their sacrificial duties barefoot. Rav Chaim, though, had a pair of special boots.

Rav Chaim always kept these high coarse farmer's boots in the corner of his private study. Such boots were out of character with Rav Chaim's normal manner of impeccable dress. Out of respect for their rabbi and teacher, his students never asked him why he kept such boots in his study.

At the Volozhin Yeshiva, the students' dormitories were approximately one hundred yards from their central study hall, the *Beit Midrash.* One morning, after a particularly heavy snowfall, Rav Chaim put on his heavy boots and walked from the dormitory to the *Beit Midrash.* To the astonishment of his students, upon reaching the *Beit Midrash,* he turned around and walked back to the dormitory. He continued to walk back and forth from the dormitory to the *Beit Midrash* until he had cleared a path in the snow for his students to walk.

HEARING YOUR OWN VOICE

1. Did you ever have a teacher express such concern, or perform acts of kindness, for you? For others?
2. What might this act of the "Brisker Rav" reflect about his approach or philosophy of education?
3. Have you ever performed an act of kindness with any of your clothes? What is your most special article of clothing?
4. *Ayeka?* What is one change you are waiting to make in your clothing habits? What is holding you back from making it?

Ki Tissa

Leadership of the Heart and the Mind

Forty days after arriving at Mount Sinai, forty days after seeing the voices and hearing the shofar, the Jewish people danced around a golden calf. They could not wait for Moses to descend from the mountain; they could not bear to remain without a leader. "And when the people saw that Moses did not come down from the mountain, the people congregated around Aaron and said to him, 'Get up, make us gods which shall go before us; for this man Moses that brought us up out of the land of Egypt, we do not know what has become of him'" (Exodus 32:1).

This failing, tragic and grievous as it was, is not altogether surprising. Once again, the Jewish people fell victim to the impatience of their childhood (see *"Beshallach"*). Amid their many crises, a momentary lapse and return to the practices of idolatry that were part of their experience in Egypt is not entirely shocking and is, perhaps, even inevitable.

The more pressing question: What is the correct response to the demand of "make us gods"? How should their leaders have

167

responded not only to the flagrant betrayal of loyalty to God, but also to the violation of the second commandment heard so recently, "You should have no other gods beside Me"?

Aaron and Moses provide two very different models of response. Moses' brother, Aaron, is thrust directly into the dilemma of responding to the demand to "make us gods." Seemingly without a moment of hesitation or a word of protest, Aaron directs the Jews to "break off the golden earrings which are in the ears of your wives and sons and daughters and bring them to me" (Exodus 32:2). Aaron subsequently fashions the gold that he receives into a calf. After the people see the calf and proclaim, "These are your gods, Israel, which brought you up out of the land of Egypt" (Exodus 32:4), Aaron builds an altar and announces that "tomorrow is a holiday for God" (Exodus 32:5).

Why did Aaron, the High Priest, acquiesce so readily to the egregious demands of the people?!

Unlike Moses, Aaron had always coexisted with his brethren. He had been a slave with them during their affliction in Egypt and he remained with them while Moses ascended Mount Sinai. He realized that the people, having been led into the desert by Moses only to see him disappear several weeks later, were filled with apprehension and terror. The people did not know how long Moses would be on Mount Sinai; from their vantage point, he had simply disappeared: "We do not know what has become of him." Aaron understood what they had endured and recognized the limits of their newly found freedom. The people were much too vulnerable to grapple with this uncertainty. For years, as slaves, their lives had been determined for them; now they were prematurely thrust into the unknown, expected to cope with the void of leadership and security.

The commentators explain that Aaron's plan was not to acquiesce to their demands; rather, he sought to delay an impending rebellion of the people. First, assuming a natural reluctance of people to part with their precious possessions, he instructed them to bring their gold and that of their families. To further deter them, he declared that they could only worship the golden calf "tomorrow." Of course, Aaron understood the gravity of their actions and consequently bore a measure of culpability for assisting them: as we find later in the Torah, God punished Aaron for his behavior. "And the Lord was very angry with Aaron" (Deuteronomy 9:20). Nevertheless, Aaron was aware of the overall context of the situation of the Jewish people; his caring for his people was so great that he was even willing to sacrifice a degree of his own innocence to try to help them. The Mishnah states that one should strive to be like "the students of Aaron, loving and pursuing peace." Aaron is regarded as the prototype of love and compassion for others.

Moses, however, had not shared this experience of subjugation with his people. Separated at childhood, he grew up as a prince in Pharaoh's palace and grew to manhood as a shepherd in the desert (see "*Shemot*: Slavery and Freedom"). Now after forty days of exalted solitude on Mount Sinai, at the very moment of the giving of the tablets, he is told by God, "Go down, because your people have become corrupt" (Exodus 32:7). Moses descends, breaks the tablets, burns and grinds the golden calf, and then forces the people to drink the ashes of the idol that they had made. He unceremoniously rebukes Aaron and calls out, "Who is on the side of God?" (Exodus 32:26). The Levites respond to the challenge and proceed to kill three thousand men who instigated the idol worship.

Moses does not tolerate a moment of concession to the needs of the people. Moments later Moses will plead with God not to destroy the whole people, but his first response is that those directly responsible must be unequivocally punished. There is no room to consider extenuating circumstances. He is unwilling to become reconciled to the limits of this slave people.

In the *parsha*, we see two responses: Aaron responds within the context of the present reality, he accepts human limitations and expresses his love for the people; Moses acts apart from their reality, he demands the transcending of present constraints and teaches truth to the people. Aaron responds from his heart; Moses, from his mind.

The Midrash asks, "Where is wisdom found? Rabbi Eliezer says: 'in one's head,' Rabbi Joshua says: 'in one's heart.'" The mind and the heart – two centers of life, two centers of wisdom, both indispensable.

HEARING YOUR OWN VOICE

1. Why did Aaron mold the gold into the shape of a calf? Rabbi Samson Raphael Hirsch speculated that Aaron wanted to choose a symbol of childishness and weakness. What do you think?
2. Which contemporary leaders do you think are more similar to Aaron's form of leadership? To Moses' leadership? What happens when only one approach exists?
3. With which style of leadership do you most identify? Why?
4. *Ayeka?* What change could you make to develop a healthier balance between your mind and your heart?

Shabbat Lunch

Persistence

Tragedy strikes the Jewish people. After forty days atop Mount Sinai, Moses descends from the mountain, sees the people dancing around the golden calf, and casts down the tablets of the Ten Commandments. The tablets, symbolizing an engagement ring, have been broken; the relationship between God and the Jewish people has been jeopardized. Moses will have to plead for forgiveness for the people and then once again ascend Mount Sinai, eventually to return with a second set of tablets.

The Jewish people did not know how long Moses intended to remain on Mount Sinai. They did not know, originally, that he was ascending for forty days. He had simply disappeared, without food and provisions. Barely seven weeks out of Egypt and suddenly leaderless, the Jewish people eventually suffered a loss of nerve, a collapse of faith and hope in Moses' return.

Apparently God kept Moses up on Mount Sinai until the Jewish people faltered and resorted to idolatry. Why? Why couldn't God have had Moses descend with the first set of tablets just a bit earlier, before the Jewish people lost their will and fashioned the golden calf? What was accomplished by having Moses ascend Mount Sinai a second time, to return with the second set of tablets?

There is a critical difference between the first and second experiences of Moses on Mount Sinai. The Torah states that the first set of tablets "were the *work of God.*" Miraculous in nature. For the second set, however, God told Moses to carve the two tablets of stone *himself.* The first set of tablets was a gift; the second set required Moses to do the work himself.

Furthermore, the first time Moses ascended Mount Sinai, every step was new, every moment a new experience of exhilaration. But what about the second time? A repeated experience never carries with it the thrill and excitement of the first time. What was the second climbing of Mount Sinai like for Moses? Every step he had already traveled, every sight he had already seen. It was a climb of mission and purpose but, perhaps, bereft of the spiritual euphoria that had accompanied the first ascent.

But therein lies the greatness of Moses and, consequently, of the Jewish people: the strength to climb the mountain a second time. Moses discovered the wherewithal not to give up, not to despair, even after crisis and tragedy, to somehow locate the resources to climb the mountain a second time. The first set of tablets was a gift. It is very difficult to fully appreciate a gift. The second set of tablets was the product of difficult but sincere human labor and persistence. Only *these tablets* would remain intact.

HEARING YOUR OWN VOICE

1. It is written in the Talmud that Moses ascended the mountain for a second time forty days before Yom Kippur and then descended with the second tablets on Yom Kippur. What might this symbolize?

2. What other figures or historical examples exemplify the quality of persistence? Do you think that one can develop this attribute in oneself or in others?

3. The breaking of the first tablets and the hewing of the second tablets are a symbol for all of life's endeavors. Have you ever persisted in "climbing the mountain a second time"? When? Why?

4. *Ayeka?* What helps you recover after a moment of brokenness?

Seuda Shlishit

Defender of the People

When the Jewish people sinned in making the golden calf, God threatened to destroy them completely. "And the Lord said to Moses, 'I have seen this people, and, behold, it is a stiff-necked people: now therefore let Me alone, that My wrath may burn against them, and that I may consume them: and I will make of you a great nation'" (Exodus 32:9–10). Moses does not accede to God's request; instead, he defends the people and fights on their behalf. "And Moses besought the Lord his God, and said, 'Lord, why does Your wrath burn against Your people, whom You brought forth out of the land of Egypt with great power, and with a mighty hand?... Turn from Your fierce anger, and relent of this evil against Your people'" (Exodus 32:11–12).

Three thousand years later, another major figure would appear who was known for his unrelenting defense of the righteousness of the Jewish people. Rabbi Levi Yitzchak of Berditchev, one of the major Hasidic leaders of Polish Jewry, was known for his great and unconditional love for all Jews. He epitomized the Hasidic trait of always finding a "spark of goodness" in all people, despite their outward behavior. He was noted for saying, "No one has the right to say anything evil about the Jewish people, only to intercede for them." The following stories are told about him:

Once Rabbi Levi Yitzchak encountered two Jews, smoking publicly on the Sabbath. He approached them and, in a gentle tone, remarked that they had obviously forgotten that it was the Sabbath. "No," they replied, "we are perfectly aware that today is the Sabbath." "Then you must not know that it is prohibited to smoke on the Sabbath," continued Rabbi Levi Yitzchak. Again they replied, "No, we are perfectly aware that it is forbidden to smoke on the Sabbath." Thereupon Rabbi Levi Yitzchak raised his hands toward the heavens and called out, "Master of the Universe, see what an honorable and virtuous people you have! Twice these Jews could have falsely replied to me, but You see, your people are only capable of telling the truth."

Even while confronting God, Rabbi Levi Yitzchak would not desist in his defense of the Jewish people. In the middle of his prayer, Rabbi Levi Yitzchak once exclaimed, "Lord of all the world! There was a time when You went around the world with that Torah of Yours, and were willing to sell it at a bargain, like apples that have gone bad, yet no one would buy it from You. No one would even look at You! And then we took it! Because of this I want to propose a deal. We have many sins and misdeeds, and You have an abundance of forgiveness and atonement. Let us exchange! But perhaps You might agree only to an even exchange? In that case, my answer is, 'Had we no sins, what would You do with Your forgiveness?! So you must balance the deal by giving us life and children and food in addition!'" (*Tales of the Chassidim*, p. 209)

HEARING YOUR OWN VOICE

1. After the sin of the golden calf, God offered to Moses to make a new nation from him. "And the Lord said to Moses, 'I have seen this people, and, behold, it is a stiff-necked people, now therefore let Me alone, that my wrath may burn against them, and that I may consume them, and I will make of you a great nation'" (Exodus 32:9–10). Why do you think that Moses did not accept God's offer to make a new nation from him? Do you think that God would actually have destroyed the Jewish people, or was this only a test to see how Moses would respond?
2. Rav Kook wrote, "Hate stems from an overabundance of self-love." Do you agree? What prevents people from focusing on the "sparks of goodness" in others?
3. Do you know anyone who always seeks to find something positive in others? What effect does this person's attitude have upon others? Upon him- or herself?
4. *Ayeka?* What advice would you give yourself to help you view the Jewish people more positively?

Vayakhel/Pekudei

Details of Creation

The book of Exodus ends with two *parshiyot* that focus on a similar theme and are often read together. The *parshiyot Vayakhel/Pekudei* recount the actual construction and sanctification of the Tabernacle.

Major sections of these *parshiyot* closely resemble the content and style of two previous *parshiyot, Terumah* and *Tetzaveh.* Once again, each utensil of the Tabernacle is described; once again, the clothes of the priests are specified in great detail. All that God told Moses to do in the two previous *parshiyot,* Moses now directs the Jewish people to carry out. Moses appoints Betzalel to be the primary architect of the Tabernacle, and he oversees this national endeavor through to its conclusion. Notwithstanding the significance and centrality of the Tabernacle (see *"Terumah:* The Unknowable"), the tedious repetition of so many details creates an almost burdensome monotony.

Why does the Torah repeat the instructions for erecting the Tabernacle in such detail? Since we are already familiar with all the details of the Tabernacle from the previous *parshiyot,* why doesn't the Torah simply state, "And all that God told Moses to do, so he did"?

The book of Exodus begins with the Hebrew letter *vav* ("and"), signifying its connection to the first book of the Torah, Genesis. Exodus completes and fulfills the processes begun in Genesis. Genesis begins with the creation of the world, the paradise of the Garden of Eden and then chronicles the history of the world through the events of the flood, the tower of Babel, and the choosing of Abraham. It culminates several generations later with the descent of the sons of Jacob to Egypt, who are about to become enslaved. This continuing descent, from paradise to Egypt, is reversed in the book of Exodus. The birth of the Jewish people, the giving of Torah, and the return to Israel are the building blocks for the restoration of the harmony that is lost with the exile from the Garden of Eden.

Yet this harmony, this return to paradise, will not be achieved effortlessly. Unlike God's creation of the world, accomplished through eternal, all-embracing utterances, the human process of creating a world of harmony will be realized only through a gradual and painstaking course, necessitating a countless number of minute and detailed actions. For the success of this process, there can be no grandiose illusions of power or fantasies of miraculous feats. National and universal harmony will not simply come to pass; human beings must struggle to bring it about incrementally, improving the world through small, modest steps of transformation.

Only a rare individual is able to perceive both the beauty of the overall project as well as the significance of each detail. The Torah writes that Betzalel, who was chosen to direct the building of the Tabernacle, was "filled with the spirit of God, in wisdom, understanding, and in knowledge, and in all matter of workmanship" (Exodus 31:3). His wisdom devolved to each element of workmanship. Metaphorically, the Talmud states that Betzalel had the power to see the value of individual letters as well as the value of words. Not only is harmony restored to the world through a process of countless details, but the truly wise are able to see the building of this harmony in each minute aspect of the process.

HEARING YOUR OWN VOICE

1. In the *parsha* of *Vayakhel*, the description of the construction of the Tabernacle is preceded by the statute to observe Shabbat (Exodus 35:1–3). From this juxtaposition, the rabbis conclude that the work from which we must abstain on Shabbat includes only those creative acts that were involved in the building of the Tabernacle. What additional lessons can be drawn from the juxtaposition of these two ideas?
2. Have you ever had the experience of seeing the "big picture" in a tiny moment? Have you ever engaged in a seemingly minor endeavor that you thought possessed national significance?
3. Do you know people who have great ideas yet falter when it comes to details? Have the frustrating details of a project ever prevented you from completing it?
4. *Ayeka?* In what detail/aspect of Judaism is it hard for you to see the bigger picture? How could you become more like Betzalel in that detail?

Shabbat Lunch
Healthy Growth

The book of Exodus closes with Moses calling together the Jewish people: "And Moses gathered together the entire congregation of the people of Israel" (Exodus 35:1). Instead of proceeding directly to the task at hand, the building of the Tabernacle, the entire people first have to be convened together. Then, after they have finished their work of building the Tabernacle, Moses proceeds to bless them: "And Moses saw all the work ... and Moses blessed them" (Exodus 39:43).

Apparently, their receiving of this blessing, which advanced them to a new level of spirituality, was contingent upon their coming together as one. Why was this so?

This theme of unity preceding growth echoes throughout the whole Torah. At the close of the book of Genesis, before Jacob blesses his twelve sons, he summons them: "Gather yourselves together" (Genesis 49:1). Before the giving of the Torah at Mount Sinai, the Midrash comments that the Jewish people achieved an unprecedented cognizance of their oneness. Similarly, the final mitzvah mentioned in the Torah, the commandment for everyone to write their own Torah, is immediately preceded by the mitzvah of *hakhel*, the gathering of all the Jewish people together in Jerusalem.

Why is spiritual growth dependent upon this prior condition of harmony and unity? Why is it necessary to gather everyone together before the giving of a blessing?

The rabbis chose to conclude their monumental work, the Mishnah, with the following statement: "God did not find any channel through which a blessing could be bestowed upon Israel other than *shalom* (peace)." Without *shalom*, without a harmonizing of all the various parts of the whole, there can be no blessing, no spiritual growth. The commentators indicate that any blessing that is received without the requisite equilibrium of *shalom* is not destined to be maintained. The founder of Hasidism, the Ba'al Shem Tov, compares spiritual growth to the climbing of a ladder. One must have a stable footing on each rung before climbing higher. Spiritual growth is a precarious stage of development, and, if it does not occur in a stable and healthy environment, it will most likely collapse amid calamitous consequences.

Similarly, the Talmud states that God's presence only dwells in a home that is characterized by *shalom bayit* (peace at home), and it will not dwell in a home in which there exists internal strife. A home characterized by dissension reflects the insistence and collision of particular concerns and an inability to reconcile these conflicting viewpoints through a higher unifying principle. Such a condition of dissension is antithetical to developing a more elevated spiritual state, to receiving a blessing. *Shalom*, peace, does not entail a negation of differences; rather, it entails the harmonizing of divergent perspectives through understanding the opinions and needs of others. Awareness of a greater picture and striving for *shalom* is the foundation and catalyst for lifelong growth.

Moses wants to give a blessing not to a countless number of individuals, but to the Jewish people as one. As a prerequisite for this blessing the Jewish people must be assembled together, so that it is clear that they understand the unique role that every member of the Jewish people plays in this national undertaking. Without national *shalom* there can be no national blessing.

HEARING YOUR OWN VOICE

1. The Talmud includes innumerable arguments among the rabbis. Why do you think that these are not considered to be examples of dissension?

2. The importance of achieving peace between all the individual parts as a prerequisite for receiving a blessing is true both on a collective and individual level. Have you ever known someone who tried to grow and change before harmonizing the disparate elements of his or her personality? What happened? Could this have been avoided?

3. Rav Kook wrote that a person suffers greatly and experiences profound anguish when his internal life is not "harmonized." Conversely, achieving unity and clarity of purpose accords the exhilaration of almost unlimited powers and potential. Have you ever felt either of these two experiences?

4. *Ayeka?* What piece of your life are you having a hard time integrating with the rest? What small step could you take to bring more unity to your life?

Seuda Shlishit

Building Dreams

The book of Exodus concludes with the building of the Tabernacle, which includes the construction of the menorah, the bronze and gold altars, the golden table, and the ark. For the Jewish people, who began the book of Exodus afflicted with the slavery of Egypt, the reality of their liberation and collective building must have seemed almost dreamlike. Their suffering in Egypt had once caused them to lose even the capacity to fantasize about a better world, "and they did not listen to Moses because of the anguish of spirit and the cruel bondage" (Exodus 6:9). Once, they were forced to build monuments for Pharaoh. Now they are engaged in physical building again, but as a free people, exploring the untapped potential within.

Almost a century ago, a lone figure managed to transcend the manifest reality of his world and to dream of building, together with others Jews, a model society. Theodor Herzl (1860–1904), an assimilated journalist from Vienna, sought to overcome the virulent anti-Semitism of his time through the creation of a Jewish homeland. For several years his efforts met with general disdain and ridicule by the Jewish community of Europe, typified in an episode in his fictional work *Altneuland (Old-New Land)*:

> Dr. Weiss, a simple rabbi from a provincial town in Moravia, did not know exactly in what company he found himself, and ventured a few shy remarks. "A new movement has arisen within the last few years, which is called Zionism. Its aim is

to solve the Jewish problem through colonization on a large scale. All who can no longer bear their present lot will return to our old home, to Palestine." He spoke very quietly, unaware that the people about him were getting ready for an outburst of laughter.... The laughter ran every gamut. The ladies giggled, the gentlemen smirked and roared.

Nevertheless, Herzl continued to toil ceaselessly for his vision. In 1897, Herzl convened the First Zionist Conference in Basel. A delegate later recounted, "For us, the first congress was a crisis that changed our fate. It revolutionized our entire world and divided the history of our exile into two parts, the first before the congress and the second the part that came after." Herzl himself wrote in his diary:

> Were I to sum up the Basel congress in a few words – which I must guard against uttering publicly – it would be this: In Basel I founded the Jewish state. If I said this aloud today, I would be answered by universal laughter. *Perhaps in five years, and certainly in fifty, everyone will agree.* The state is already founded, in essence, in the will of the people to be a state; yes, even in the will of a sufficiently powerful individual.

At the conclusion of his book Herzl wrote, "Dreams are not so different from deeds as some may think. All the deeds of men are only dreams at first."

HEARING YOUR OWN VOICE

1. Why do people of vision often provoke reactions of scoffing and sarcasm? Do you know anyone who has overcome the skepticism or derision of others to pursue a dream?
2. What do you think is the difference between a visionary and an eccentric or insane person?

3. What dream would you like to see fulfilled for the Jewish people fifty years from now?

4. *Ayeka?* What audacious dream animates your life?

Leviticus

Vayikra

A Call of Forgiveness

The third book of the Torah begins with the words, "And [God] called to Moses." The book of Genesis described the creation of the world, the patriarchs and the matriarchs, and the development of the twelve tribes of Israel. The book of Exodus recounted the birth of the Jewish people, the giving of the Ten Commandments at Mount Sinai, and the building of the Tabernacle. The book of Leviticus is referred to in Hebrew as *Vayikra*, "and He called." It reveals God's "calling" to the Jewish people – a call of affection, according to Rashi, summoning them to affirm their relationship with God and to live as a holy people.

Eventually, however, every relationship may suffer temporary breakdowns. In a moment of oversight, a thoughtless act may be committed, a date may be forgotten. Unintentionally, a strong bond may be weakened or even endangered. The Jewish people's relationship with God, both individually and collectively, undergoes times of crisis and strain. Then what? After a moment of broken trust, of carelessness and disappointment, how can the relationship be restored?

The first *parsha* of the book of *Vayikra*, which is also called *Vayikra*, describes several of the types of sacrifices that the Jewish people brought in the desert. Though far removed from our contemporary reality, these sacrifices represented an archetype for mending a broken relationship. Among these offerings were several sacrifices that were brought by individuals to repair their relationship with God after incidents of breakdown. "And it will be forgiven him for anything of all that he has done wherein to incur guilt" (Leviticus 5:26). Each sacrifice was accompanied by a personal admission of guilt and contrition for previous actions.

How can the process of bringing an offering be able to heal an injured relationship? How does this act serve as a paradigm for the restoration of harmony and trust?

The commentators explain that the *olah* sacrifice of this week's *parsha* atones for an act of omission, a missed opportunity to strengthen a relationship, and the Torah explicitly states that the *chattat* offering yields forgiveness for an accidental transgression. Intentional acts of malice, of course, severely damage a relationship. An act of hostility clearly reflects the desire to inflict pain upon the other person. But what does an act of forgetting or an accidental oversight express? What does a simple act of overlooking imply about the relationship? Relationships may be weakened and even destroyed through unintentional acts of carelessness. What should the response to such acts be?

The mystical book of the *Zohar* explains that sacrificing an animal is meant to convey a poignant message – that a person who has been careless, who has forgotten to perform an expected act, has, in a certain way, diminished his humanity and behaved like an animal. The ability to exercise free will and make productive decisions separates humans from the animal kingdom. Mindlessness is a symptom of an unhealthy relationship that must be set back on course. The bringing of a sacrifice serves as a powerful reminder that one must struggle to ensure that all of one's thoughts and actions reflect a conscious decision-making process and do not simply occur instinctively.

Yet there is another obstacle impeding the resumption of the relationship. Even after recognizing a mistake, it is difficult to ask for forgiveness. The person who intends to apologize may fear that the attempt to heal the relationship will be met with frustration and anger and that his "peace offering" may be rejected. In addition, the combination of guilt about having damaged the relationship and the fear that positive overtures may be repulsed may preclude someone from reaching out for forgiveness.

To alleviate these concerns, the *parsha* of *Vayikra* both begins and ends with God's calling out and offering forgiveness to man. God initiates the healing process; the Hebrew word for sacrifice is *korban*, meaning literally "a coming closer." The *parsha Vayikra* begins with God's call to come closer, to resume and heal the relationship that has been injured. It is difficult to ask for forgiveness, just as it is difficult to forgive someone who has caused pain. The paradigm created here is that the one who has been ignored and overlooked, the one who has experienced the pain (in this case, God), calls out.

"*Vayikra*" is a call of invitation, a call designed to remove the fear of rejection and to begin the process of renewal. It is a call that echoes throughout the whole book of *Vayikra*.

HEARING YOUR OWN VOICE

1. The bringing of a sacrifice is a public act. Everyone who sees it knows that the person bringing it committed an accidental transgression. What effect do you think that the public nature of the sacrifice had upon the person asking for forgiveness?
2. Now that we no longer have the daily sacrifices of the Temple, Maimonides writes that an individual's prayers have assumed

the role of achieving atonement (Laws of Prayer 1:4–6). What do you think are the positive and negative aspects of this change?

3. The paradigm of forgiveness set forth in *parsha Vayikra* is that the party who is hurt initiates the healing. Do you identify with this model of forgiveness? Have you ever had a relationship mended in a similar way?

4. *Ayeka?* Who do you need to offer an opportunity to ask for forgiveness? Which of your relationships needs you to initiate a healing process?

Shabbat Lunch

Approaches to Prayer

The *parsha* of *Vayikra* concentrates on the sacrificial system of the Temple. For the last two thousand years, however, the Temple sacrifices have been replaced by the prayer service, which takes place primarily in the synagogue. Instead of actually coming to Jerusalem, Jews now direct their hearts toward Jerusalem. The peak moment of this directing of one's heart occurs during the silent standing prayer called the *Amidah*. The Mishnah states that during the *Amidah*, even if a snake were to wrap itself around a person's leg or a king were to ask a question, one should not interrupt this moment of prayer.

What is supposed to occur during these moments of prayer? While standing in total silence, what is the one praying trying to achieve? What should one be thinking?

Among the many philosophies of prayer developed by Jewish thinkers over the last two thousand years, two radically divergent approaches can be found in the writings of Samson Raphael Hirsch, one of the leaders of German and all Western European Jewry during the nineteenth century, and Rav Kook, the first chief rabbi of the state of Israel.

Rabbi Shimshon Raphael Hirsch writes that:

> There are two Divine services: the inner Divine service [prayer] and the outer, active, Divine service [in the whirl of life]. The inner Divine service should serve as a *preparation* of the outer one and should realize, in it, its main purpose.
>
> This fulfillment of the Divine will in our inner self can come to its perfection only *by bringing about a change in our thoughts and emotions* – namely, by evoking and rejecting, and by bringing to life and reviving thoughts and emotions in our inner self.
>
> *Hitpallel* (to pray), from which *tefillah* (prayer) is derived, originally meant to *deliver an opinion about oneself, to judge oneself....* Thus it denotes to step out of active life in order to attempt to gain a true judgment about oneself, that is, about one's ego, about one's relationship to God and the world.... It strives to infuse mind and heart with the power of such judgment as will direct both anew to active life-purified, sublimated, strengthened.

For Hirsch, prayer represents a cognitive, analytical opportunity for self-judgment. Prayer is a "means," a vehicle through which people strive to examine their behavior and to find concrete resolutions for improving their course of action. The clarity and effectiveness of these insights were the signs of a successful prayer experience.

Rav Kook espouses a more mystical approach to prayer:

> Prayer is only correct when it arises from the idea that the soul is always praying. It [the prayer of the soul] flies and embraces its lover [God] without any break or separation.... The *perpetual prayer of the soul* continually tries to emerge from its latent state to become revealed and actualized, to permeate every fiber of life of the entire universe.

For Rav Kook, the moment of prayer is one of listening and connection with one's essential spiritual self. In contrast to Hirsch, Rav Kook views prayer as neither analytical nor introspective. It does not focus on evaluating one's latest behavior, nor does it serve as preparation for the outer, active whirl of life. For Rav Kook, prayer is an opportunity to filter out the multitude of voices and demands that continually monopolize one's attention and to listen to the divine voice within oneself. Every person is created in the image of God, and this "divine spark" is always speaking, communicating to the individual his or her uniqueness. During prayer one strives to hear the "perpetual prayer of the soul."

The rabbis referred to prayer as "the work of one's heart." One should experience a "change of heart," a transformation, during prayer. For both Rabbi Shimshon Raphael Hirsch and Rav Kook, successful prayer is a life-changing occurrence.

HEARING YOUR OWN VOICE

1. Organized Jewish prayer is intended to be a synthesis of spontaneous individual prayer and organized communal prayer. Can you think of any drawbacks or potential dangers of prayer experiences that possess only one of these two qualities?

2. In this unit we encountered two approaches to prayer: Rabbi Shimshon Raphael Hirsch views prayer as an analytic moment of self-judgment aimed at improving one's behavior. Rav Kook views prayer as a meditative moment of listening to one's deepest voice. With which of these two outlooks do you identify most? Can you think of an alternative approach to prayer?

3. What do you think are the major obstacles that preclude meaningful prayer experiences? How might they be overcome?

4. *Ayeka?* What small step could you take to improve your prayer life?

Seuda Shlishit

A Child's Flute

In the eighteenth century, a new movement, *Hasidut*, arose in Judaism, which stressed the centrality of prayer. Its founder, known as the Ba'al Shem Tov (1700–1760), taught that while learning and knowledge are important in the service of God, above all else, God desires the faithful devotion of one's heart (in Hebrew, *kavannah*). All else, even learning Torah and doing mitzvot, are vehicles to help generate clinging (*devekut*) to God. The following story, precariously balancing on the antinomian edge of *Hasidut*, was one of the Ba'al Shem Tov's classics.

> A villager who went to town every year on the High Holy Days to pray in the synagogue of the Ba'al Shem Tov had a son who was so simple that he could not even learn the Hebrew alphabet, much less a single prayer. And because the boy knew nothing, his father never brought him to town for the holidays.
>
> Yet when the boy reached the age of thirteen and became responsible for his actions, his father decided to take him to the synagogue on Yom Kippur, lest he stay at home and, in his ignorance, eat on the holy fast day. And so they set out together. And the boy, who had a little flute on which he used to play to his sheep, unbeknownst to his father, put the flute into his pocket.
>
> In the middle of the service, the boy, touched by the power of the prayers, suddenly said, "Father, I want to play my pipe!"
>
> The horrified father scolded his son and told him to behave himself. A while later, though, the boy said again, "Father, please let me play my pipe!" Again his father scolded him, warning him not to dare; yet soon the boy said a third time, "Father, I don't care what you say, I must play my pipe!"

"Where is it?" asked the father, seeing that the boy was uncontrollable.

The boy pointed to the pocket of his jacket, and his father seized it and gripped it firmly so that the boy could not take out his little flute. And so the hours passed with the man holding onto his son's pocket. The sun by now was low in the sky, the gates of heaven began to close, and it was time for the final prayer of the day (*Ne'ilah*).

Halfway through the closing prayer, the boy wrenched the pipe free from his pocket and his father's hands, put it to his mouth, and let out a loud blast that startled the entire congregation. As soon as the Ba'al Shem Tov heard it, he hurried through the rest of the service, as he had never done before.

Afterward, when asked by his followers why he had hastened through the remaining prayers, he told them "when this little boy played his flute, all your prayers soared heavenward at once and there was nothing left for me to do but finish up."

HEARING YOUR OWN VOICE

1. According to Jewish mysticism, the ideal way to pray is like a little child. What do you think is so admirable about a child's prayers?
2. If God is omniscient, knowing both our needs and merit, what is the purpose of prayer?
3. What was your most powerful prayer experience?
4. *Ayeka?* What would be your equivalent of the little boy's flute?

Tzav

The Source of Fire

As already noted, many of the *parshiyot* (portions) of the Torah come in pairs, with the second *parsha* expanding and deepening the ideas introduced in the previous week's *parsha*. This week's *parsha*, *Tzav*, develops themes present in last week's *parsha*, *Vayikra*, and concludes the account of the preparations necessary for the installation of the Tabernacle (Hebrew, *Mishkan*), the holy sanctuary at the heart of the camp of the Jewish people.

While there are many similarities between the two *parshiyot*, several striking distinctions should be noted. First, although both *parshiyot* concern bringing sacrifices, *Vayikra* dealt with the offerings brought by *individual* members of the Jewish people, whereas *Tzav* discusses the sacrifices brought by the priests (*kohanim*). The sacrifices brought in *Vayikra* were primarily voluntary offerings brought *after an individual had sinned*, as an expression of his desire to repair a damaged relationship with God. In contrast, the *olah* sacrifices, which the *kohanim* were commanded to bring at the beginning of *Tzav*, were to be brought daily, at sunrise and sunset, *regardless of the behavior or inclinations of the kohanim*. The *olah* (meaning "to go up") is the only sacrifice that is completely burnt in the altar, whereas all the other sacrifices have parts that are permissibly eaten either by their owners or by the *kohanim.*

In addition, the beginning of this week's *parsha* repeatedly emphasizes the fire that burned continuously on the altar, "It is the *burnt* offering, which shall be *burning* upon the altar all night until the morning, and the *fire* of the altar shall be kept *burning* in it. And the *kohen* shall … take up the ashes which the *fire* has consumed with the *burnt* offering…. And the *fire* upon the altar shall be kept *burning* in it; *it shall not be put out.* And the *kohen* shall *burn* wood on it every morning…. The fire shall ever be *burning* upon the altar, *it shall never go out*" (Leviticus 6:2–6).

The "continual fire" was the source of all fire in the Tabernacle. From it, the lights of the Menorah, the fire of the altar, and all other fires were kindled. Yet even after all the other fires were lit or when there was no need to light fires from it – that is, when this fire served no practical function – the *kohanim* were still commanded to maintain it. It was prohibited to extinguish even one ember of this fire, since the Torah states "it shall never go out."

The Torah forbids the wanton destruction of any element of nature, yet aren't the daily burning of the *olah* sacrifice and the continual fire on the altar examples of waste? Are these two examples of destruction, or is there a creative process and intention underlying these acts?

Both these cases of apparent destruction and waste can be resolved by a single, unifying principle. The Tabernacle, physically placed at the heart of the Jewish encampment, symbolized the heart of the Jewish people. Just as the heart pumps blood to all parts of the body, so too, every quality of the Jewish people emanated from this central source. The health and purity of the heart ultimately determine the well-being of the whole organism.

How does one maintain a healthy, pure heart? The Midrash states that the *olah* offering was a force of purification, brought exclusively to "purge impure meditations of the heart." It served as a daily reminder for the *kohanim* (and consequently for all the Jewish people) to prevent their innermost thoughts from wandering and becoming corrupt or commonplace. Similarly, the continual fire, when seen in the context of the Temple environment, was supposed to remind its viewers of the need to eradicate, or to burn away, all nonessential and dispensable thoughts.

The Tabernacle (and subsequently the Temple) were not places of magic. Ultimately they were structures that enabled the human beings working in them to elevate and transcend their physical realities. Later in Jewish history, many of the prophets bewailed that the services occurring in the Temple were empty acts, bereft of spiritual intent. The degree to which the *kohanim* were focused on their tasks determined the worthiness of the entire Temple existence. Thus the continually burning fires and the daily reminder of the burnt *olah* offering helped to keep the meditations of all who saw them properly directed. In the end, as the Talmud states, "God desires [the purity and sincerity of] one's heart."

HEARING YOUR OWN VOICE

1. Unlike Greek mythology, in which Prometheus was punished for stealing fire from the gods, the Torah affirms the human use of fire and directs the Jewish people to continually burn fires in their holy places. What might this difference indicate about the different approaches of Greek mythology and Judaism regarding the relationship between God (or the gods) and humanity?

2. The Hasidic master S'fat Emmet explains that there are two kinds of fire: fire that consumes and fire that gives light. Can you think of examples of this paradigm in Judaism? In personal growth and/ or relationships?

3. The fire continually burning was supposed to excite and vitalize all those who saw it. Which aspect of Judaism makes you the most enthused?

4. *Ayeka?* What part of your Jewish identity has lost its fire? What could you to do reinvigorate it?

Shabbat Lunch

Vegetarianism

This week's *parsha*, *Tzav*, deals with the Temple animal sacrifices, some of which were completely burned upon the altar and some of which were eaten by either the *kohanim* (priests) or the owner of the animal. Rav Kook writes that in the messianic age, all sacrifices will be vegetarian, brought from either flour mixtures or plants (*Olat HaRa'ayah*, p. 292).

Does this imply that, in the future, the human diet will also become vegetarian? Is there either a Jewish imperative to eat meat or an inclination toward refraining from eating meat products? On what grounds would Judaism advocate a vegetarian diet?

Originally, in the Garden of Eden, man was given permission to eat only seed-bearing herbs and fruits. In this garden paradise, which included no trace of death, man could eat only foods that carried within them the powers of creating further life.

Ten generations later, after the flood, Noah was given permission to eat animals. "Every moving thing that lives will be food for you; just like the green herb have I given you all things" (Genesis 9:3). Humanity's relationship with the animal world was drastically altered. The previous harmony was shattered. Now "the fear of you and the dread of you will be upon every beast of the earth, and upon every bird of the air, and upon all that moves upon the earth" (Genesis 9:2). The primary limitation placed upon humanity now was the prohibition of eating the blood of an animal.

The third stage of human-animal relations occurred after the Jewish people's exodus from Egypt, during the forty years of their wandering in the desert. Now the Torah prescribed that every time one wanted to eat meat, the animal had to be brought to the Tabernacle at the center of the camp to be slaughtered. The proximity of the killing of the animal to the place of greatest holiness imbued the physical act of slaughtering with a sense of holiness and raised the act of eating to a spiritual plateau.

The fourth and final stage occurred when the Jewish people entered the Promised Land. Moses tells the people, "When the Lord your God will enlarge your border ... and you will say, 'I will eat meat,' because you long to eat meat; then you may eat meat to your heart's desire" (Deuteronomy 12:20). Once in the land of Israel, the Jewish people were allowed to eat meat whenever and wherever they wanted, without the stipulation of bringing the animal to the place of greater holiness.

In his work *The Vision of Vegetarianism and Peace*, Rav Kook writes of the paradoxical nature of Jewish vegetarianism. According to Rav Kook, the moral ideal is to refrain from harming all animals. He notes that the verse that gives permission to the Jewish people to eat meat in Israel also subtly infers a concealed disdain for this inclination. The emphasis upon, "and you will say, 'I will eat meat,' because *you long to eat meat*" implies that God allowed the Jewish people to eat meat only as a concession to their insatiable "heart's desire." He writes that the reason that Jewish law requires us to cover up the blood spilled of a slaughtered animal is to hide our shame over having desired to eat the animal in the first place. The day will come, he writes, when every human being will feel a natural repulsion over spilling the blood of an animal, and the world will evolve to a more sensitive and developed moral plane.

On the other hand, Rav Kook strongly cautions against the displaying of great kindness for animals at the expense of directing kindness toward other human beings. The human arena should always remain our primary focus. Only those who have developed a high degree of compassion in all of their life's engagements should seek to actualize this level of mercy toward animals.

It is told that Rav Kook ate a tiny morsel of meat on Shabbat to symbolize both the yearning for the vegetarianism of the Garden of Eden as well as the awareness that we have not yet achieved this status and must not delude ourselves that the world has already attained an advanced moral level. The result of living this paradox deepens the longing to advance and perfect this world.

HEARING YOUR OWN VOICE

1. In contrast to Rav Kook, who sees meat eating as a concession to human desire, Jewish mystical works view the ingestion of an animal as the greatest kindness one can perform, because in eating the animal, a person elevates its nature from the animal to human, and thus elevates the animal to a higher spiritual plane. What do you think?
2. According to Jewish law, an *am ha'aretz* (an ignorant, boorish person) is prohibited from eating meat (*Pesachim* 49b). Why do you think that this is so?
3. Are you or have you ever considered becoming a vegetarian? For what reasons?
4. *Ayeka?* What could you do to elevate and sanctify your eating habits?

Seuda Shlishit

Compassion for Animals

Though *Tzav* deals primarily with the sacrificing of animals, both the letter and spirit of the law in Judaism stress the compassion that one should always extend to all creatures. The Talmud (*Bava Metziah* 85a) records that almost two thousand years ago, the leader of the Jewish people, Rabbi Judah HaNasi (the head of the Sanhedrin), was punished for an uncompassionate act and then, because of his kindness, was forgiven.

Once, a calf was being brought to slaughter. It ran away and placed its head in the corner of Rabbi Judah's robe, and cried pitifully. Rabbi Judah said to it, "Go [to your slaughter], for this is why you were created."

At that time it was declared [in heaven], "Since Rabbi Judah showed no compassion for the calf, let grief and misfortune come upon him."

His suffering was removed because of a compassionate act: One day, the maidservant of Rabbi Judah was sweeping his home. She found baby weasels lying there and was about to sweep them out. Rabbi Judah said to her, "Leave them, for it is written, 'And His [God's] compassion is for all of His creations'" (Psalms 145:9).

At that moment it was declared [in heaven], that "since he was merciful, let us be merciful with him," and his grief and misfortune were removed.

HEARING YOUR OWN VOICE

1. The Talmud (*Eruvin* 100b) states in the name of Rabbi Yochanon: "If the Torah had never been given, we would have learned modesty from the cats, not stealing from the ants, faithfulness from the dove, and courting rituals from the chicken and rooster." What else do you think one might learn from animals?
2. While owning and caring for pets may be a sign of compassion for animals, it may also lead to caring for animals at the expense of caring for human beings. What do you think are the pros and cons of having pets?
3. What is the greatest act of compassion toward animals that you have performed? That you have witnessed?
4. *Ayeka?* What did the story of Rabbi Judah evoke in you?

Shemini

An Obsession with the Holy

Tragedy strikes. The very first episode of human initiative in the book of Leviticus ends in calamity. Just like the Torah's description of the Garden of Eden, in which Adam and Eve spend preciously little time in paradise before the onset of crisis and expulsion, so too, in this week's *parsha* the joy of the Jewish people is regrettably brief. On the eighth and final day of the erection of the Tabernacle, people bring sacrifices, Moses and Aaron bless the people, a miraculous fire from heaven accepts their offerings, and the people rejoice.

In the very next verse, tragedy strikes. A heartbreaking drama ensues seconds after this moment of exultation, as Aaron's eldest sons, Nadav and Avihu, are struck down while entering the Tabernacle to burn their incense offering. "And Nadav and Avihu, the sons of Aaron, took each of them his censer, and put fire in it, and put incense on it, and offered *strange fire* before the Lord, which He had not commanded. And a fire went out from the Lord, and devoured them, and they died before the Lord" (Leviticus 10:1–2).

One moment the Jewish people are jubilant, and the next moment there are no words to describe this dreadful loss. "And Aaron was speechless" (Leviticus 10:3).

What happened? What possessed Nadav and Avihu to offer this "strange fire" that "God had not commanded"? Weren't they aware of both the sanctity and hazard surrounding the Holy of Holies?

Nadav and Avihu were the prospective leaders of the generation after Moses and Aaron. They alone had been singled out by name at Mount Sinai to ascend with Moses and Aaron. "And God said to Moses, 'Come up to the Lord, you and Aaron, Nadav and Avihu, and the seventy elders of Israel'" (Exodus 24:1). The Midrash explains that they had been selected to eventually replace Moses and Aaron, yet because of an apparent flaw in their leadership qualities, they would never fulfill their destiny.

What was the fatal shortcoming of Nadav and Avihu? They offered a "strange fire," which was "strange" because it had not been commanded by either God or Moses. Why would they have dared to break the rules of the Tabernacle and ostensibly enter without having been invited by either God or Moses?

According to the Midrash, Nadav and Avihu brought the "strange fire" because they were intoxicated! The future leaders of the Jewish people, the next in line to be the High Priest in the Tabernacle – drunk?! The Midrash arrives at this conclusion based upon the fact that the next section of the Torah (Leviticus 10:8–11) prohibits priests from drinking wine or strong drink while performing their service. "And the Lord said to Aaron, saying, 'Do not drink wine or strong drink, neither you nor your sons with you, when you enter the Tent of Meeting [Tabernacle], lest you die.'" The startling juxtaposition of the deaths of Nadav and Avihu with this restriction against drinking is the probable basis for the Midrash's assertion.

Nevertheless, the answer of the Midrash begs the question: Why was there concern that the priests might drink wine to excess? We do not find such prohibitions with regard to the judges, prophets, or other public figures. Why was the Torah only worried about intemperate drinking of priests in the Tabernacle or the Temple?

The rabbis understand that wine possesses a liberating quality that sometimes leads to disgraceful behavior but can also enable a person to reach spiritual heights. The Talmud established that Kiddush, *Havdalah*, weddings, circumcisions, and other holidays should all be accompanied by the drinking of wine. "The rabbis taught, [it is written] 'Remember the Sabbath day and make it holy.' Remember it through [the drinking of] *wine*" (*Pesachim* 106a). The drinking of wine temporarily frees people of their personal inhibitions and thus may enable them to come more in touch with their spiritual identity.

What might have happened to Nadav and Avihu? Inspired by the celebrations of the people and in ecstasy over the completion of the Tabernacle, the future leaders of the Jewish people may have been overtaken by their spiritual fervor. Their passion for holiness brought them to disregard the known strictures of the Tabernacle and violate the boundaries of the "Holy of Holies." Their fervent passion to become closer to God was ultimately self-destructive.

The Tabernacle, the very place that was supposed to be the source of life, brought about the death of two of the people's leaders. In the shadow of tragedy, Aaron becomes voiceless. His emptiness reverberates throughout the whole community. The lesson of the dangers of uncontrolled individual passion has been taught to the Jewish people.

HEARING YOUR OWN VOICE

1. One of the possibilities suggested by the Talmud to explain the nature of the "Tree of Knowledge of Good and Evil" in the Garden of Eden is that it was a grapevine. Given what is known about wine, why do you think that this possibility was suggested?

2. Sometimes an impulsive act does not occur as an isolated circumstance but rather represents the actualization of certain qualities or tendencies long present in an individual. The

only other information about Nadav and Avihu that the Bible discloses is that they did not have any children. The Midrash infers from this that neither of them ever married. There is a tradition that one should not begin the study of Kabbalah (mystical tradition) until one is married. What do you think is the rationale for this? Could there be a connection to the fates of Nadav and Avihu?

3. Have you ever known someone whose enthusiasm for a project or work has caused him or her to lose sight of "the bigger picture"? What were the consequences? How did the person regain a healthier perspective of his or her undertaking?

4. *Ayeka?* In the continuum from extreme passion to extreme self-control, toward which side do you lean? How do you find balance?

Shabbat Lunch

Yuhara

And Nadav and Avihu, the sons of Aaron, took each of them his censer, and put fire in it, and put incense on it, and offered strange fire before the Lord, which He had not commanded. And a fire went out from the Lord, and devoured them, and they died before the Lord. (Leviticus 10:1–2)

Nadav and Avihu were punished for conducting themselves beyond the letter of the law. They were spiritually gifted though fervently independent personalities, and they died while attempting to scale previously unprecedented spiritual heights. The Talmud ascribes a number of different causes for their deaths. Among them, the Talmud states that Nadav and Avihu sought to express their religious beliefs regardless of preexisting social norms and did not confer respect to their generation's leaders. "They instructed rulings of law while in the presence of Moses, their teacher" (*Eruvin* 63a).

Should one's religious behavior be limited by preexisting social norms? Does expressing oneself independently necessarily constitute a problem? Can religious conformism and social pressure become negative influences and thwart personal growth?

The Mishnah (*Berakhot*, chapter 2) discusses a potential conflict between personal religious inclinations and the prevailing communal custom. Although it is a mitzvah to recite the *Shema* every night, special exemption is given to a bridegroom on his wedding night, because the rabbis assume that he will be so overtaken with excitement and tension that he will not be able to recite the *Shema* with its proper level of concentration. What if, nevertheless, the groom feels that he will be able to control himself and that he will not be distracted by his nervousness, and he chooses to recite the *Shema*? Should he be allowed to recite it, or should he be forced to yield to the accepted custom of exemption

The Mishnah concludes with Rabbi Shimon ben Gamliel's statement that "not all that choose to take the '*name*' should (be allowed to do so)." This "name" that not all are allowed to take is the appellation reserved for one who is commonly regarded as having extraordinary piety in all of one's behavior. Only one who is already recognized by the community as having achieved a very high spiritual level should be allowed to forgo this exemption and recite the *Shema* on one's wedding night. For anyone else, this would be considered an act of hubris, of exaggerated or false religious devotion. The rabbis wanted to inhibit spiritual pretension and affectation.

They wanted to deter sporadic, ostentatious exhibitions of piety and to limit immoderate flourishes of religious grandiosity. They created a legal category, referred to in Hebrew as *yuhara* (literally, "making a mountain of oneself"), to prohibit such displays of religiosity. The rabbis were aware that spiritual devotion could be motivated by a desire for attention, behavior intended to create the impression of honor and righteousness. Any religious behavior that is not commensurate with one's recognized conduct and position within the community is suspect of being self-serving and possibly pompous. Public forms of prayer were considered to be especially susceptible to acts of *yuhara*, and excessive bowing, standing for the entire service, or choosing to stand next to the rabbi were all considered to be haughty expressions of religiosity.

This category of *yuhara* is intended to serve as a moral check for the Jewish society, impelling each individual to build an integrated life of spirituality, harmonious with his or her community. Nadav's and Avihu's instructing while in the presence of their own teacher, Moses, reflect their desire to use Torah to advance their personal standing within the community. Their greatest legacy is a warning against acts of *yuhara*.

HEARING YOUR OWN VOICE

1. Why might religious observance be especially prone to exaggerated public displays of spirituality?
2. The Talmud states that a blessing only resides with one who does kind acts in private. Why do you think this is so?
3. Have you ever witnessed any incidents of *yuhara* in Jewish life?
4. *Ayeka?* Has your "ego voice" ever directed an act or behavior in your Jewish life? When was the last time? If you could talk to your "ego voice," what would you say to it?

Seuda Shlishit

Painting a Shul

This *parsha*, *Shemini*, describes the dedication of the Tabernacle, the structure erected by the Jewish people that would serve as the channel for receiving God's blessing. After Moses and Aaron came out of the Tabernacle and blessed the people, "the Glory of God appeared to all of the people" (Leviticus 9:23). Ever since the destruction of the Second Temple, for almost two thousand years, Jews have tried to make synagogues places of blessing and sanctity.

The Rebbe of Ruzhin was the head of a prominent Hasidic dynasty. When the time had come to repaint his shul (synagogue), a contest was held to see who would be the most worthy of receiving the honor of painting the Rebbe's shut. Hundreds of artists demonstrated their talents. Finally, four were chosen. It was decided that each artist would be given one wall to work on and two weeks to complete his task.

The first artist painted a mural of the story of Creation.

The second artist painted the giving of the Torah at Mount Sinai.

The third artist depicted the coming of the Messiah and the World to Come.

The people of the town were very excited. Never before had a shut been decorated with such vivid and inspiring pictures. They all wondered how the fourth artist could possibly match the works of his three predecessors.

The fourth artist walked into the shut and sat down, staring at the other three scenes. He sat there for one day, and then another day, for three days, a week, and then for ten days. People began to whisper, "He will never finish, he doesn't know what to do. Maybe he should not have been chosen." The artist continued to sit and gaze at the walls.

All of a sudden, the artist stood up, and in a frenzy started to work on his wall. He finished it in one day.

It was Friday night. Everyone was ready to receive of Shabbat. The Rebbe of Ruzhin walked into the shul. He looked around, admiring the work of all four artists. Then he turned toward his hasidim, and said, "All the artists are wonderful, but the fourth artist is the most precious Jew in this town."

On his wall, he had created a mirror that reflected the work of the other three artists. His creativity had included the creativity of all the others.

HEARING YOUR OWN VOICE

1. If you were assigned to paint a mural on a synagogue wall, what would you paint?
2. Eight hundred years before the dynasty of the Rebbe of Ruzhin, Maimonides objected to murals and mosaics that might distract the worshiper during the prayer experience. What do you think is the role of aesthetics in the experience of prayer?
3. What synagogue or setting have you found to be the most conducive to your praying?
4. *Ayeka?* Where is the creativity in your spiritual life? What small step could you take to bring more creativity to your spiritual or prayer life?

Tazria/Metzora

Dealing with Loneliness

The two *parshiyot* (portions) of *Tazria* and *Metzora* are often read together during the yearly cycle of Torah readings. Prior to these *parshiyot*, the structure of the Jewish camp has been established and certain guidelines have been established to ensure its stability (see *"Shemini"*). The Holy of Holies is at the center of the encampment, surrounded by three concentric rings of public domain. The precisely detailed arrangement of the camp enables the twelve tribes and the individuals therein to understand their roles in maintaining the purity and holiness of the nascent Jewish society. A model community based on personal uniqueness, mutual respect, and balanced cooperation is in the process of being achieved (see *"Vayechi"*).

Yet no human society functions without crises and breakdowns. Now that the system of the community has been instituted, the *parshiyot* of *Tazria* and *Metzora* detail a number of individual cases that threaten to dissolve the order and harmony of the Jewish people. The central personalities of these *parshiyot*, the new mother and the leper, both have to leave their families, suffer temporary exile (either outside their homes or outside of the Holy of Holies), and finally bring a sin-offering sacrifice before they are allowed to return to their homes and rightful places in the camp.

At first glance, the title figures of these two *parshiyot* could not seem more different. The first, the birthing mother epitomizes a life-giving force. After carrying life within her for nine months, she now has brought a new being into the world. In contrast, the second title figure, the leper (*metzora*), experiences a form of living death. His skin turns deathly white, his hair falls out, his body is plagued with ghastly afflictions.

In addition, the origin of their conditions seems to be utterly dissimilar. The birthing woman, having brought a new life into this world, has not only performed a wholly natural and positive act but has helped to fulfill the first mitzvah given to humanity, namely, to "be fruitful, multiply, and replenish the earth" (Genesis 1:28). The leper (*metzora*), however, suffers the consequence of sinful or aberrant actions. His leprosy is, in fact, a physical expression of a moral shortcoming, as the Midrash ascribes numerous causes of leprosy (*tzara'at*), ranging from idolatry to selfishness. The most common cause of leprosy mentioned in the sources and commentators is *lashon hara* (gossip or slander). The two other incidents of *tzara'at* in the Torah both occur in the contexts of improper speaking about other individuals.

Why, then, are these two seemingly disparate cases juxtaposed? What offense has the new mother committed to warrant exile? Moreover, why should the birthing mother and the leper share the similar fates of having to leave their places of abode and bring sin offerings before they are allowed to resume their previous lives?

They seem to be reflecting physical states resulting from entirely different circumstances. Yet at their source, the new mother and the leper have both experienced profoundly similar emotional states.

The Talmud (*Niddah* 31b) states that the new mother must bring a sin-offering after having given birth because in the midst of her birth pains, she swears that she will never return to her husband, so as to preclude repeating the agony of childbirth. At the most intense moment of childbirth, the mother screams a scream of utter loneliness, of emotional isolation. No one can understand her pain; no one is able to share the depths of her mood or spirit. It is her experience alone.

The *metzora* (leper) has spoken *lashon hara*. His punishment is to dwell entirely alone, outside of the camp, until he has been cured. His punishment befits the transgression of gossiping, as the one who defamed and thus divided the community must now sense the very same loneliness. One of the primary motivations for speaking *lashon hara* is the need to bond and discover a way to relate with others. The loneliness one feels impels him or her to speak negatively about others, to search for any possible means of connection.

The new mother and the leper have both experienced moments of heartfelt loneliness. This sense of loneliness may ultimately have debilitating effects on the functioning of the Jewish community, as it potentially undermines the family relationships and social cooperation vital to a healthy society. Eventually the mother will need to return to her husband. Eventually the leper needs to develop productive ways to interact with other members of society. Their feelings of loneliness should not remain scarring moments, haunting them forever. The fabric of society cannot afford to be weakened by their feelings, no matter how natural or justified they may be. To be enabled to confront and move beyond these experiences, both these personalities must temporarily leave their homes and undergo periods of actual separation, of loneliness.

Tragically, one rarely truly appreciates something until it has been lost. The temporary "losing" of their former place amid the Jewish camp hopefully instills in the new mother and leper a greater desire to return and become productive members of their society. Their recent traumas of loneliness should ultimately serve to bond them with those whom they have left.

HEARING YOUR OWN VOICE

1. Another explanation for the new mother's bringing of a sin offering is that the sin offering is a response to a form of "spiritual postpartum depression." The exhilaration of carrying life and bringing a new being into this world may be followed by a severe emotional letdown, an anticlimactic return to reality. Do you think that moments of depression or gloom naturally follow emotional peaks?

2. The Talmud (*Moed Katan* 5a) states that when people would come near to the leper, he was supposed to call out, "Impure, impure," thus imploring them to pray for him. How else do you think that this would influence his healing?

3. How do society or families today enable individuals to overcome their experiences of loneliness? What mechanism(s) would you suggest to help facilitate this? Have you ever found loneliness to be beneficial?

4. *Ayeka?* Who in your family or community do you think may be lonely? What gesture could you make to help alleviate their loneliness?

Shabbat Lunch

Seeing One's Moral Self

The Torah's obsession with the *metzora* (leper) is difficult to understand. Over one hundred verses describe the physical symptoms of the *metzora*, ranging from the swelling and discoloring of the skin, to spots, sores, and baldness. There seems to be an inordinate detailing of the sickness and healing of the *metzora*.

The commentators are quick to clarify that the *tzara'at* (leprosy) of the Torah should not be confused with the medical disease of leprosy, more likely known in the Torah as *shcheen*. The *metzora* was not examined by a doctor but by the *kohen* (priest). The Talmud posits that no one was declared a *metzora* on Shabbat, holidays, or during wedding celebrations, the times of greatest social gatherings, since *tzara'at* was not contagious.

What did this person do that he became afflicted with *tzara'at*? The Talmud states that the cause of *tzara'at* was the speaking of *lashon hara* (gossip). The rabbis of the Talmud ask, "Why is the *metzora* different [from all other transgressors] that he must dwell utterly alone, outside of the inhabited camps?" Because he caused a division (estrangement) between husband and wife, and between friends [through his gossiping]; therefore, the Torah demanded that he now must remain alone. The Talmud continues, "Rabbi Yehuda ben Levi said, 'Why is the *metzora* different that he must sacrifice two birds upon becoming pure? The Torah demands of one who has performed an act of "chirping" (*lashon hara*), that he must bring a "chirping" sacrifice'" (*Erchin* 16b).

Why did the *metzora* become so ugly? Why is it necessary that we are informed of the gruesome details of the *metzora's* plague? The ugliness of the *metzora* is not a punishment, rather, a reflection of his true self. The physical symptoms of *tzara'at* serve as a mirror of the person's moral repulsiveness. The *metzora* is forced to stare at the dissolution of his physical self with the understanding that it signifies his moral dissolution. The detailed picture drawn by the Torah of the *metzora* emphasizes the agony that he must endure, knowing that his entire community witnesses the outcome of his moral failings. Amid physical and emotional pain, the *metzora* himself is visited by the ugliness of his actions. Ultimately, the goal is not to punish the *metzora* but to have him repent.

Apparently, in the time of the Temple, the most effective way to convey this message was to actually see the consequences of one who spoke *lashon hara*. Today, hopefully, this lesson is learned through reading of the frightful fate of the *metzora*, who was guilty of not guarding his tongue.

HEARING YOUR OWN VOICE

1. Why do you think that *lashon hara* was deemed such a serious crime by the rabbis?

2. Do you think that one's physical appearance is affected by one's moral behavior? Did you ever physically feel beautiful (or ugly) because of something that you did?

3. If you could see your moral self, what would be your most beautiful quality? Your most ugly quality? If you could see the moral appearance of others, who would be the most beautiful person whom you know? Why?

4. *Ayeka?* What is one small step you could take to become more spiritually beautiful?

Seuda Shlishit

Acher's Brit Mila

In the book of Genesis, Abraham was ninety-nine years old when he had his *brit mila* (circumcision), and his first son, Yishmael, was circumcised at thirteen. In this week's *parsha*, the Jewish people are told to circumcise their sons on the eighth day after birth. The *brit mila* represents the first public act between the parent and the child.

The Jerusalem Talmud (*Chagigah* 7b) records the ill-fated *brit* and rite of passage of Elisha ben Abouyah.

Elisha ben Abouyah is almost never referred to by his name in the Talmud. He is simply known as *Acher*, the "Other." A student of Rabbi Akiva, he forsook the Jewish way of life and became the foremost apostate of the Talmud. The Jerusalem Talmud attributes the source of his apostasy to a declaration made by his father at his *brit mila*.

Elisha's father, Abouyah, was one of the most notable personages in Jerusalem. On the day of his son's *brit*, Abouyah invited all of the important figures in Jerusalem and seated them in one room. In a second room, he seated Rabbi Eliezer and Rabbi Yehoshua. The guests began to eat and drink, to sing and dance. Rabbi Eliezer said to Rabbi Yehoshua, "While they are engaging in their world, let us engage in ours."

The two rabbis began to learn and discuss matters of Torah. After discussing the Five Books of Moses, they discussed the Prophets, and then the rest of the Holy Writings. Fire descended from the heavens and encircled them. Abouyah said to them, "Rabbis, what are you doing?! Have you come here to burn my house down?" They replied to him, "Certainly not. We were sitting and reviewing words of Torah, and then the Prophets, and then the holy Writings. And the words were as blazing as when they were given at Mount Sinai, and, just as at Mount Sinai, the letters were surrounded by fire. As it is written, 'and the Mountain blazed with fire up to the heavens.'"

Abouyah said to them, "Rabbis, if this is the power of Torah, then for the whole life of my son, I will dedicate him to Torah."

Since Abouyah's intention was not pure, the Torah learning of his son did not last.

HEARING YOUR OWN VOICE

1. What was wrong with Abouyah's response? What do you think would have been the proper response to the rabbis' learning of Torah and the descending of fire?
2. Can you offer several reasons why his father's declaration might have led Elisha ben Abouyah to eventually go astray?
3. Why do you think that the Talmud considered it especially important that the motivation for learning Torah be "pure?"
4. *Ayeka?* What small step could you take to refine your motivation for learning and Jewish behavior?

Acharei Mot

Returning to Life

The opening verse of *Acharei Mot*, "And the Lord spoke to Moses after the death of the two sons of Aaron, when they approached before the Lord, and died" (Leviticus 16:1), seems superfluous and unrelated to the rest of this week's *parsha*. The deaths of Nadav and Avihu have already been described in *Shemini* (see "*Shemini*: An Obsession with the Holy"). We already know what happened to them. Furthermore, the continuation of this week's *parsha* is, on the surface, unconnected to their fate. Nevertheless, the death of Nadav and Avihu serves as an introduction to this *parsha*, becomes the title of the *parsha* (*Acharei* Mot: "After the Deaths"), and somehow sets the theme that will affect everything that comes thereafter.

Why does this week's *parsha* begin with this seemingly unconnected statement about the deaths of Nadav and Avihu? How is their fate relevant to this week's *parsha*?

Acharei Mot is composed of three chapters, each with a distinct theme:

1. The service of the High Priest on Yom Kippur (chapter 16).
2. The regulations of eating meat and personal sacrifices (chapter 17).

3. The defining of the sexual mores of the Jewish people (chapter 18).

Each of these topics has been dealt with briefly in previous sections of the Torah. *Tetzaveh* outlines the clothing and sacrificial duties of the priests; *Shemini* enumerates forbidden foods, and *Tazria* specifies the laws regulating the new mother. In this week's *parsha*, however, these three subjects are linked together for the first time. The majority of the laws of the first of these topics, Yom Kippur, concern the service of the High Priest. Yet one enigmatic command is also directed to the Jewish people: "You shall afflict your souls" (Leviticus 16:29). The Torah repeats this command a number of times, never explicitly defining what this "afflicting of souls" entails.

The Mishnah (*Yoma* 8:1) clarifies the nature of these afflictions: "On Yom Kippur it is forbidden to eat, drink, wash, anoint oneself, wear [leather] shoes, and have sexual relations." These six restrictions are arranged in three pairs, depicting three categories of life. Eating and drinking are necessary for an individual's *physical* survival. Washing and anointing are requisite for the *social* domain of human interaction. Though perhaps less obvious, the prohibitions against wearing of shoes and sexual relations can be seen as referring to the *spiritual* realm – at his encounter with the burning bush, Moses is ordered, "Do not come near: take your shoes off your feet, for the place upon which you are standing is holy" (Exodus 3:5). Because of its potential to bring a new soul into this world, the Mishnah understands that sexual relations possess the sanctity of the Holy of Holies.

Though Yom Kippur is often understood primarily to be a day of fasting, these additional prohibitions reflect a more powerful and inclusive message: Yom Kippur is a day dedicated to the total cessation of human activity and creation, on which the physical, social, and spiritual drives are denied. Affliction is thus the suspension of all growth. The day of affliction, the holiest day of the year, is essentially a day of death.

The next two chapters of *Acharei Mot* return us to the most powerful physical drives propelling humanity: eating and sexual relations. Immediately after scaling the spiritual heights of Yom Kippur, the day of transcending human needs, the Torah returns to the reality of human existence. The step away from life must serve, ultimately, as a catalyst and invitation to return to the passions of life, now attuned with greater moral and spiritual refinement.

Returning to the original question: Why did *Acharei Mot* begin with a flashback to the fate of Nadav and Avihu? The entire *parsha* is read in the shadow of their deaths. Nadav's and Avihu's spiritual passion eclipsed their physical worlds. The lesson of Yom Kippur can only be properly understood "after the death of the two sons of Aaron, when they came near before the Lord, and died" (Leviticus 16:1). The experience of Yom Kippur is not an end, in and of itself, rather the vehicle through which the Jewish people are able to better sanctify their very human, physical realities.

Only after reminding us of the deaths of Nadav and Avihu can the afflictions of Yom Kippur occasion a day of death that enhances and empowers life.

HEARING YOUR OWN VOICE

1. The rabbis of the Talmud expanded on the Day of Atonement of the Torah and transformed it into a day of utter cessation of creation, simulating one's death. Why do you think they decided that this was its most appropriate form of expression?

2. Maimonides divided his encyclopedic work of Jewish law, the *Mishneh Torah*, into fourteen books. In the book entitled *Kedusha* (Holiness), he included only the laws of eating and sexual relations. Why do you think that he did this?

3. Do you think that more fully developing one's spiritual qualities necessarily diminishes one's physical life? Have you ever seen examples of this?

4. *Ayeka?* Have you ever had a near-death experience? How did it affect you?

Shabbat Lunch

Modes of Change

And this will be an eternal statute for you, that in the seventh month, on the tenth day of the month, you will afflict your souls, and do no work. (Leviticus 16:29)

This week's *parsha, Acharei Mot,* details the procedure of Yom Kippur, the Day of Atonement. The ultimate goal of this day is to serve as a catalyzing force for change.

Why should an individual change? Does this presuppose that there is something wrong with him or her? Furthermore, how does this change, or the awareness for the need to change, transpire?

The Torah presumes that every individual possesses both free will and an infinite potential for development. Not only does every individual have the capacity for change, but change is intrinsic and essential to his or her very being. Rav Kook understood that the human being was part of the evolutionary process (not to be confused with Natural Selection, which includes humanity's development from the monkeys) of the world, and that periods of stagnation deny the natural growing process of life. He wrote that "the doctrine of evolution that is presently gaining acceptance in the world has a greater affinity with the secret teachings of the Kabbalah Jewish mysticism] than all other philosophies. Why shall we not compare the events of general existence to the events in the life of an individual person or any other creature?" Change does not need to happen because of some shortcoming in the individual. The world is in a continuous stage of evolution, and therefore, in order to be in harmony with the world, the individual must also continually develop and grow.

There are a multitude of forces, ranging from physical to emotional to spiritual, which may encourage a person to make a change in his or her life. Regardless of the actual change at hand, Rav Kook writes that change most likely occurs in one of two forms, sudden or gradual.

1. Sudden change comes about as a result of a certain *spiritual lightning bolt* that enters the soul. At once the person senses ... that he has become a new being; already he experiences inside himself a complete transformation for the better. This form of change dawns on a person through some inner spiritual force whose sources are entirely mysterious.

2. There is also a gradual form of change. No sudden flash of illumination dawns upon the person to make him change for the good, but he feels that he must mend his way of life, his will, his pattern of thought. By heeding this impulse he gradually conditions himself to becoming a good person, reaching higher levels of purity and perfection. (*Lights of Repentance,* chapter 2)

The first process of change, sudden change, is intuitive and inexplicable. It is the result of a sudden awareness, an epiphany or realization, that the person cannot quite fathom yet understands is personally true. This insight is given neither to articulation nor to reasonable explanation, yet it resonates convincingly within the individual. The second process of change, gradual change, lends itself to rational formulation and evaluation. Incrementally, the person examines his or her life and judiciously determines whether his or her path is progressing in a beneficial direction, at a healthy pace.

Rav Kook's two processes of change have their origins in the two sources of life within the individual: the heart and mind. Both the heart and the mind continually push for growth and greater life. These two sources express themselves in the drives for sudden (*heartfelt*) and gradual (*rational*) change. A life of growth results from listening to and synthesizing both these voices.

HEARING YOUR OWN VOICE

1. Rav Kook wrote that a deep understanding of the process of evolution should bring about a perpetually optimistic outlook on life. Why?

2. In the excerpt previously quoted, Rav Kook writes of a "spiritual lightning bolt." Elsewhere, he writes that "each time that the heart feels a truly spiritual stirring, each time that a new and noble thought is born, we are as though listening to the voice of an angel of God who is knocking, pressing on the doors of our soul, asking that we open our door to him." Have you ever experienced this kind of heartfelt inspiration?

3. Rav Kook describes two different kinds of change: sudden and gradual. With which of these two processes do you most identify? Do you know someone who typifies the other process?

4. *Ayeka?* What title would you like to give to the next chapter of your life?

Seuda Shlishit

On the Verge of Conversion

This week's portion, *Acharei Mot*, details the Temple service performed by the High Priest on Yom Kippur. In the time of the Temple in Jerusalem, the practices of Yom Kippur included the special service of the High Priest, the sacrificing of animals, and the sending out of the scapegoat. Though none of these practices have been observed since the destruction of the Temple in the year

70, the power and spiritual intensity of Yom Kippur has continued to change the lives of countless Jews nonetheless.

When Franz Rosenzweig (1886–1929) was twenty-seven years old, he made the necessary preparations to convert to Christianity. Rosenzweig had been raised in a minimally Jewish home, and a number of his friends and relatives had already left Judaism. On July 7, 1913, he himself finally made the decision to convert. Rosenzweig, destined to become one of the leading Jewish theologians of Western Europe, resolved not to enter Christianity without any religious identity but rather to come to it as a Jew. He would fulfill this intention by attending Yom Kippur services in Berlin later that year.

Rosenzweig never completed his plan of action; he never converted to Christianity. Instead, his life was forever changed by his experience during the Yom Kippur services that he attended in Berlin. Several days later, he wrote to his mother, "I seem to have found the way back, about which I had tortured myself in vain and pondered for almost three months." Many years later he would write, "Anyone who has ever celebrated the Day of Atonement knows that it is something more than a mere personal exaltation, or the symbolic recognition of a reality such as the Jewish people; it is a testimony to the reality of God which cannot be controverted."

In 1921, Franz Rosenzweig completed his magnum opus, *The Star of Redemption*. Writing on postcards from his bunker during World WAR I, Rosenzweig blended the concepts of humanity, the universe, and God, with the themes of creation, revelation, and redemption, and formed them into a single coherent Jewish philosophy. After World WAR I, together with Martin Buber, Erich Fromm, Gershom Scholem, and other notable German intellectuals, Rosenzweig helped to found the "Free Jewish House of Learning," which was a paradigm and center of Jewish learning for its duration.

In *The Star of Redemption*, Rosenzweig wrote that on Yom Kippur, "man is utterly alone ... everything lies behind him ... he confronts the eyes of his judge in utter loneliness, as if he were dead in the midst of life."

For Franz Rosenzweig, on his momentous Yom Kippur of 1913, everything did indeed "lie behind him." From that moment on, his new life commenced.

HEARING YOUR OWN VOICE

1. Prior to his Yom Kippur experience, Franz Rosenzweig wrote that one of the shortcomings of Judaism (or of Jews) was its lack of passionate faith. Would you agree?

2. Rosenzweig wrote "Everything earthly lies so far behind the transporting into eternity during this [Yom Kippur] confession, that it is difficult to imagine that a way can lead back from here into the cycle of the year." Did you ever experience anxiety or find it difficult to return to life after Yom Kippur?

3. Did you ever have a life-changing moment on Yom Kippur? Do you know anyone who did?

4. *Ayeka?* What was one change you made in your life during the last year?

Kedoshim

Spiritual Masters

As has already been noted, the *parshiyot* (portions) of the Torah often come in twosomes. In such instances, the first *parsha* establishes the basic ideas, while the second develops and deepens the themes presented in the first. The previous *parsha*, *Acharei Mot*, set the essential minimal boundaries for acceptable social behavior. Now *Kedoshim* will attempt to advance this standard to higher and more profound levels.

"And the Lord spoke to Moses saying, 'Speak to all the congregation of the children of Israel and say to them, "You shall be holy, for I, the Lord your God, am holy"'" (Leviticus 19:1–2). At Mount Sinai, God promised the Jewish people that they would become a "holy nation" (Exodus 19:6). Now each person is individually commanded to fulfill this calling. They are not summoned to become "good," or "honorable," or "especially worthy." They are required to become "holy."

Only recently the Jewish people had been slaves in Egypt. What were they supposed to think when they were now told to become "holy"?! At this moment in history, what did "becoming holy" mean to the Jewish people?

223

Rashi understands this directive as referring to the minimal standards governing eating and sexual behavior introduced at the end of last week's *parsha*. He writes that by virtue of adhering to these strictures one necessarily becomes "holy." The call to become holy does not carry with it new patterns of actions; rather, it describes the state attained through the fulfillment of the laws previously conferred.

Commenting on Rashi's explanation, the Ramban understands that becoming "holy" extends beyond the eating and sexual regulations mentioned in *Acharei Mot*. Ramban writes that a person can satisfy all the particulars of these laws (by not eating prohibited foods and not engaging in sexual relations proscribed by the Torah) and still demonstrate loathsome behavior through *excessively indulging* in his or her physical drives. The challenge of "becoming holy" is reflected in the exertion of self-control precisely within the guidelines set by Torah law. One should not eat immoderately or yield unrestrainedly to one's sexual drive. This type of conduct reflects being an "abomination within the domain of Torah law."

For the Ramban, the call to become "holy" is the Torah's setting of a standard that goes beyond the "letter of the law." Where laws no longer reign, where the authority of society is unable to demand compliance, there individuals are exhorted to master themselves and to become "holy."

According to this understanding of the Ramban, could one ever actually become "holy?" Can one ever totally master the proper involvement and direction of one's physical drives?

Other religions and cultures have understood the concept of "holiness" to involve some form of detachment from this-worldly behavior. "Holy" people lead ascetic lives entailing the denial of physical commitment and pleasure. In such clearly defined circumstances, holiness becomes attainable – one becomes holy through relinquishing certain patterns of behavior. Obliterating certain drives may, in fact, be easier than trying to sustain and direct them.

According to the Ramban, the challenge of living a holy life involves continually aspiring to neither deny nor become controlled by one's physical drives. The question is not "Is this act allowed or prohibited?" but rather, "Although permitted, am I at this moment expressing the fact that I have been created in the image of God?" In last week's *parsha*, the "letter of the law" prohibitions concerning eating and sexual behavior were established. The separation of these two *parshiyot* reflects the assumption that the human being develops in stages. In *Acharei Mot*, one is commanded to discriminate between permitted and proscribed behavior. Then in *Kedoshim* one is charged to perpetually elevate the realm of behaviors that are technically allowable.

The question of last week's *parsha* was "Is it allowed or not?" Now the question is "Is it holy?"

HEARING YOUR OWN VOICE

1. According to the Ramban, how a person spends his or her spare time would be a strong indicator of his or her true character. Why? Do you agree?
2. According to one of Rav Kook's foremost students, Rav Harlap, there is a subconscious voice in each individual trying to convince him or her not to improve, not to try and become more "holy." Do you agree? Have you ever felt this?
3. Is there anyone whom you would call *kadosh* (holy)? Why?
4. *Ayeka?* During the past year, has there been any behavior on your part – whether in act, thought, or speech – that you feel was holy? What comes to mind?

Shabbat Lunch

Commanding Love

"And you will love your neighbor as yourself ... " (Leviticus 19:18).
Two thousand years ago, Rabbi Akiva said that this maxim was
the guiding rule of the entire Torah. This commandment has been
quoted by an untold number of religions and cultures. Yet there
remains a very disturbing and enigmatic dimension to this commandment: How can the Torah presume to command an emotion?

Aren't emotions, by their very nature, beyond the dictums of
one's control? How can the Torah tell me to love someone whom
I do not love? For those whom one already loves, there is no need
for a commandment; rather, it is precisely to those whom one does
not naturally like or love that this commandment refers. How can
the Torah assume that a human being will be able to love everyone?

Over one hundred years ago, Samson Raphael Hirsch, one of
the leading rabbis of Western Europe, offered this commentary:

> The loving of our neighbor as we love ourselves is practically
> impossible to carry out ... (rather) we are to rejoice in his good
> fortune and grieve over his misfortune as if it were our own. We
> are to assist at everything that furthers his well-being and hap-
> piness as if we were working for ourselves, and must keep trou-
> ble away from him as assiduously as if it threatened ourselves.
> This is something which does lie within our possibilities and
> is something which is required of us – even toward somebody
> whose personality may actually be highly antipathetic to us....
> Nobody may look upon the progress of another as a hindrance
> to his own progress, or look on the downfall of another as the
> means for his own rising, and nobody may rejoice in his own
> progress if it is at the expense of his neighbor.

Hirsch understood that this verse was not directing a person to
bond emotionally with other people but rather to act as if he loves

the person and to outwardly care for all other beings-something that does lie within an individual's control.

In his discussion of the commandment "And you will love the Lord your God," Maimonides equates a person's love with his or her level of knowledge of the other. "According to the level of knowledge will be the level of one's love, if a little – then a little, if a lot – then a lot" (Laws of Repentance 10:6). The demand to love is instructing one to learn more about each person. If one finds the actions of another to be loathsome, then one must strive to understand the possible origins and reasons for such behavior. This deeper knowledge and perception of the other will engender greater empathy and positive feelings.

The Hasidic masters, epitomized by the S'fat Emmet, also grappled with the problem of commanding one's emotions. They offer a third and uniquely Hasidic resolution:

> The philosophers challenge this idea and say, "How is it possible to command love? Isn't love an abstract idea which is depen-dent on the nature of the person; can a person love simply by virtue of being thus commanded?"
>
> However, the answer is inherent in this question. Because the verse commands us to love, we must conclude that it is potentially possible for each individual to love, if only he does what is necessary to arouse this love.

According to this approach, one's love for another is primarily a function of one's own ability to love. Each person must develop and expand his or her own capacity to love. If they fully develop their loving potential, then people will be able to love all beings.

Countless interpretations have been offered to resolve the ques-tion of the commanding of love. Hirsch focuses on one's external behavior; Maimonides equates love with knowledge of the other; and the S'fat Emmet believes that loving another begins with one's own ability to love. These three thinkers represent three prototypes of this guiding rule of Torah, "Love your neighbor as yourself."

HEARING YOUR OWN VOICE

---

1. In context, the commandment of "love your neighbor" reads as follows: "Do not take revenge and do not hold a grudge against the children of your people, love your neighbor as yourself, I am the Lord." How are the other parts of this verse connected to loving one's neighbor?

2. Why do you think that the commandment is not to "love your neighbor," rather that one should "love your neighbor *as yourself*"? What understanding of human nature do these two additional words add?

3. With which of these three previously mentioned approaches do you most identify? Do you know anyone who typifies a different approach of love? How do you resolve the problematic nature of commanding an emotion?

4. *Ayeka?* Who is the most loving person you know? What can you learn from this person?

Seuda Shlishit

Silent Acquiescence to Sin

It is very difficult to criticize one's friends or peers. Nevertheless, this is the command presented in this week's *parsha:* "Do not hate your brother in your heart, you *must certainly reprove your peer,* and do not bear sin on his account" (Leviticus 19:17). (See "*Vayigash*: Giving and Taking Advice.") The Talmud (*Shabbat* 54b) states, "Anyone who could possibly have prevented someone from transgressing and does not prevent it will eventually receive the punishment for that sin." One's lack of protest or rebuke upon seeing an immoral act is tantamount to the approving of that act. The Talmud (*Gittin* 55b–56a) relates a tragic example of this type of silent acquiescence:

The destruction of Jerusalem came through Kamtza and Bar Kamtza. A certain man had a friend named Kamtza and an enemy named Bar Kamtza. He once made a party and said to his servant, "Go and bring Kamtza." The man went and brought Bar Kamtza [by mistake].

When the man [who gave the party) found him there he said, "Aren't you my enemy! What are you doing here? Get up and leave!"

Said the other, "Since I am here, let me stay, and I will pay you for whatever I eat and drink."

He said, "No."

"Then let me give you half the cost of the party." "No," said the other.

"Then let me pay for the whole party."

He still said, "No." He took him by the hand and put him out.

Said Bar Kamtza, "Since the rabbis were sitting there and did not stop him, this shows that they agreed with him. I will go and inform against them to the government."

He went and said to the emperor, "The Jews are rebelling against you." He said, "How can I tell?' He said to him, "Send them an offering and see whether they will sacrifice it [on the altar]." So he sent with him a fine calf. While on the way, he [Bar Kamtza] maimed its upper lip, or some say on the white of its eye, in a place where we Jews] consider it to be unfit for sacrificing but the non-Jews do not.

The Talmud concludes that because the Jews would not offer the sacrifice, the emperor thought that they were rebelling. Consequently, the Temple was destroyed, its sanctuary was burnt, and the Jewish people were exiled from their land.

HEARING YOUR OWN VOICE

1. Why do you think that the rabbis did not intervene on Bar Kamtza's behalf at the party? Why do you think that the Talmud

ascribed the destruction of Jerusalem to the failure of the rabbis present at the party to reprove the host?

2. Do you think the host could have done anything to restore the damaged honor of Bar Kamtza? What?

3. Do you know of any examples of religious or political leaders who have publicly reproved others even though it endangered their popularity?

4. *Ayeka?* Have you ever "stood by" instead of "standing up"? What small step could take to become more pro-active in circumstances that call you to "stand up"?

Emor

Cycles in Time

These are the special days of the Lord, holy gatherings, which you should proclaim them at their special times. (Leviticus 23:4)

Emor introduces a list of the major holidays of the Jewish calendar. While in the previous *parsha*, *Kedoshim*, the Jewish people had been instructed to become a holy people, now they are charged to recognize and observe holiness in time. Prior to this week's *parsha*, the Jewish people had been told to observe Shabbat, Rosh Chodesh (the new moon), and Passover. But now for the first time, they are told to observe all the major festivals: Passover, Shavuot, Rosh Hashanah, Yom Kippur, Sukkot, and the eighth day of Sukkot (which was considered to be an independent holiday).

Although this week's *parsha* lists the full roster of biblical Jewish holidays, later in the Torah, in the book of Deuteronomy, the list of holidays include only Passover, Shavuot, and Sukkot, with no mention of Shabbat, Rosh Hashanah, or Yom Kippur. The three holidays of Passover, Shavuot, and Sukkot thus seem to comprise a distinct unit and cycle of time.

What distinguishes Passover, Shavuot, and Sukkot from the other special days of the Jewish calendar?

Passover, Shavuot, and Sukkot are unique in that they each reflect historical, agricultural, and national realities.

Historically, these three holidays each reflect a significant event in the development of the Jewish people: Passover celebrates the Jewish people's exodus from Egypt, Shavuot traditionally commemorates the giving of Torah at Mount Sinai, and Sukkot recalls God's care for the Jewish people during their wandering in the desert.

Agriculturally, Passover is celebrated during the time of planting in the spring. The Torah refers to its time of celebration as the month of *Aviv* (Deuteronomy 16:1), the springtime. Shavuot is called "the holiday of the firstfruits (*bikkurim*)" (Numbers 28:26), as it is celebrated at the time of the first harvest. Sukkot is celebrated at the time of the major harvest, as the Torah says, "You shall observe the feast of booths seven days, in your gathering of your grain and wine" (Deuteronomy 16:13).

On a national level, in Deuteronomy, all three of these holidays are described as pilgrimage holidays, being fully observed only in Jerusalem: "Three times a year shall all the males appear before the Lord your God in the place which He shall choose; in the holiday of the unleavened bread [Passover], in the holiday of weeks [Shavuot], and in the holiday of booths [Sukkot]" (Deuteronomy 16:16).

Furthermore, the progression between these three holidays reflects a paradigm of growth in the relationship between the Jewish people and God. Passover, the first of these holidays, commemorates the birth of the Jewish people and the beginning of their relationship with God. The Passover Seder accordingly focuses on children, as we see from the four questions, the four types of sons, and so forth. The seven-week period between Passover and Shavuot represents the springtime of the relationship between God and the Jewish people, that is, the period of youth. Shavuot represents God's betrothal of the Jewish people, with the giving of the Ten Commandments symbolizing an engagement ring. Finally, this relationship between God and the Jewish people reaches adulthood during the holiday of Sukkot. The *sukka* (booth) symbolizes a *chuppa* (wedding canopy), as the relationship between God and the Jewish people is consummated.

Within this national cycle of time is woven another cycle, from Rosh Hashanah until Yom Kippur, which reflects a process of individual of growth and change. One opinion in the Talmud understands Rosh Hashanah as commemorating the sixth day of Creation, the day on which Adam and Eve were created. Thus on Rosh Hashanah we remember the moment of creation of the human being and not a specifically Jewish historical event. The ten days from Rosh Hashanah until Yom Kippur are referred to as the "ten days of repentance," signifying a process of personal, individual introspection and growth.

The ten days of repentance between Rosh Hashanah and Yom Kippur interrupt the national cycle of events from Passover through Sukkot. When taken altogether, the interweaving of these two cycles forms an annual drama of personal and national growth. At Passover and Shavuot the Jewish people's relationship with God is created and developed. Yet before there can be ultimate national bonding (the wedding of Sukkot), each Jew has to focus and amend his or her individual life. Only then, as individuals and as a nation, are we ready to culminate this relationship at Sukkot. Thus it comes as no surprise that, although there is an obligation to rejoice on all the holidays, only on Sukkot, the culminating holiday of these two cycles, does the Torah state that we should be completely happy, "*v'hayeetem ach sameach*" (Deuteronomy 16:15).

HEARING YOUR OWN VOICE

1. Do you relate more to the national or individual aspects of the Jewish holidays?
2. During the rabbinic period, Hanukkah and Purim were added to the Jewish calendar. In the last fifty years, a number of new

holidays have entered the Jewish calendar: Israel Independence Day, Jerusalem Day, and Holocaust Remembrance Day. Have you found ways to make these days meaningful?

3. Which holiday of the calendar is the most significant for you? Which custom of that holiday do you appreciate most? Why?

4. *Ayeka?* What small step could you take to make the next holiday more personally meaningful?

Shabbat Lunch

The One Not Chosen

This week's *parsha* deals primarily with two subjects: the special status of the *kohanim* (priests) and the holidays of the Jewish calendar. Both the priests and the special days are referred to as being holy, *kadosh*. In addition, the Torah relates that priests who have suffered certain bodily injuries may not enter the most holy *kadosh* places of the Tabernacle. Thus found in this *parsha* are distinct levels of holiness in person, place, and time.

The selection of the *kohanim* enabled a percentage of the Jewish people to focus exclusively on sacred matters, without the pressures of earning a livelihood and owning land. A reciprocal relationship existed between the *kohanim* and the Jewish people: in return for the community providing their physical sustenance, the *kohanim* provided spiritual guidance and direction for the nation.

The choosing process, however, is always fraught with dangers and complications. By definition during the selection process, someone has not been chosen; someone has been left out. How will this person feel about not having been chosen?

Throughout the Torah, the choosing of a person has almost always resulted in feelings of animosity toward the person who was chosen. In the book of Genesis, God chose Abel's offering and rejected that of his brother Cain, resulting in Cain's becoming distraught and killing his brother. When Jacob chose Rachel over her sister Leah, the result was "... and the Lord saw that Leah was hated...." (Genesis 29:31). Though the Torah never states that Jacob hated Leah. Jacob's choosing of Rachel engendered feelings of being hated within Leah. Similarly, the strife between Joseph and his brothers resulted from Jacob's choosing of Joseph. "And when his brothers saw that their father loved him more than all of his brothers, they hated him" (Genesis 37:4).

The problematics involved in choosing can be found not only within families, but also among nations. The rabbis understood that God's choosing of the Jewish people aroused the animosity of the other nations. The Talmud (*Shabbat* 89a) derives this from a subtle play on the words *Sinai* and *sin'ah* (hatred): "Why was it called 'Mount Sinai?' Because it was at that mountain, when the Jewish people were chosen, that the hatred (*sin'ah*) of the other nations for the Jews came into the world."

The blessing given to Abraham was that "in you all the families of the world shall be blessed" (Genesis 12:3). Ultimately, the hope of the Jewish people is to convey to the nations of the world that their being chosen was not a rejection of the other nations but was intended to bring benefit and blessing to them.

HEARING YOUR OWN VOICE

1. Perhaps partly to avoid arousing feelings of animosity, the *kohanim* were known for their love of the Jewish people. Before giving their benediction to the people, they would say a blessing stating that they should "bless the people in love." Can you think of any examples from the Torah (or from life), in which someone was separated out and did not incur hatred? How was this accomplished?

2. Why do you think that not being chosen provokes antagonism?

Why do you think that this hostility is directed toward the one chosen, rather than the one who chooses?

3. Have you ever resented someone else for being chosen?

4. *Ayeka?* What does the expression "Chosen People" bring up for you?

Seuda Shlishit

Moshe the Cobbler

This week's *parsha, Emor,* describes the major holidays of the Jewish calendar, Passover, Shavuot, Rosh Hashanah, Yom Kippur, and Sukkot. The discussion of these holidays is preceded by a reminder to observe Shabbat, the weekly holiday on the Jewish calendar: "Six days will work be done; but the seventh day is the Sabbath of solemn rest, a holy gathering; you will do no work; it is a Sabbath to the Lord in all your dwellings" (Leviticus 23:3).

A story is told of Moshe the cobbler and his efforts to refrain from work on Shabbat.

> There was once a poor cobbler named Moshe. Moshe felt he had nothing of value in his life. He had never really accomplished anything: his shoes never came out right, there was never enough food in his house, he would never be a scholar. It seemed that anything that Moshe touched was doomed to fail. Everyone knew that poor Moshe was one of those people who would never succeed, and, in his heart of hearts, Moshe knew this more than anyone else.
>
> One Friday night, after singing Kiddush off-key, and then having the most modest of meals, Moshe and his wife went to sleep.

Suddenly, in the middle of the night, Moshe's wife was woken up by the joyous singing and dancing of her husband. "Moshe," she screamed, "What's gotten into you?"

"I just had a dream," he replied. "A most wonderful dream. I dreamt that a messenger from the king had knocked on my door and told me that I had just been appointed to be the head of the king's army, that I would wear silken robes with medals, ride in a golden chariot, and that everyone would have to honor me, just as they honor the king himself. I asked the messenger, 'Is there anything that I have to do?' and he replied, 'Only to check the troops.'

"I asked him, 'How often do I have to review the troops?' and he told me for just fifteen minutes every day. 'Every day?' I asked. 'Yes,' he replied.

"'Even on Shabbat?' 'Yes,' he replied. 'Every day for fifteen minutes.' Then I told him that I was deeply honored, but that I would have to refuse. How could I work even for one minute on Shabbat?"

At this point, Moshe's wife could no longer control herself. "Moshe, why are you singing and dancing?!! Even in your dream you didn't succeed; you didn't take the job!"

Moshe turned to her and smiled, perhaps the first real smile of his life: "Don't you see, my dear, I'm singing and dancing because now I realize that I really do have something of value in my life. Something that is even more precious than all the honor in the king's kingdom."

HEARING YOUR OWN VOICE

1. What do you think gave Moshe the strength to resist the king's offer?
2. How do you think that refraining from working on Shabbat affects one's life during the other six days of the week?

3. Do you know anyone like Moshe the Cobbler, someone who has not achieved external success but who has found "something that is even more precious than all of the honor in the king's kingdom?" What did they find? What would it be for you?

4. *Ayeka?* What advice would you give yourself for making Shabbat more meaningful and joyous for you?

Behar Bechukkotai

A Closing of Hope

The two *parshiyot Behar/Bechukkotai* are often read together as one unit. Together they close the book of Leviticus, which began with the voice of God calling to Moses out of the Tabernacle in the heart of the camp.

How would we have expected this book to end?

The *parsha Behar* enumerates the laws of the Sabbatical (seventh) year and the Jubilee (fiftieth) year, and stipulates the caring for the poverty-stricken.

> *"When you come into the land which I give you, then the land will keep a Shabbat to the Lord.* Six years you will sow your field, and six years you will prune your vineyard and gather in its fruit; but in the seventh year the land will have a *Shabbat Shabbaton,* a Shabbat for the Lord, you will not sow your field or prune your vineyard ... And you will count for yourself seven *Shabbatot* of years, seven years seven times, and you will have the space of seven *Shabbatot* of years, forty-nine years ... *And if your brother grows poor, and his well-being fails while with you, then you will strengthen him."* (Leviticus 25)

Contrary to what might have been expected at the end of Leviticus, there is no mention of sacrifices, no reference to the Tabernacle or the priests; rather, the uniquely Jewish laws of land ownership and social commerce are described. During the seventh year, all debts would be remitted and the land would lie fallow. During the Jubilee year, most of the land that had been sold during the previous forty-nine years would be returned to its original owner, and Jewish slaves would go free. The shofar would be blown, the year would be sanctified, and the economic organization of the Jewish people would be restored to its original and natural condition. Those who had become poor could once again garner hope that their plight would be relieved and that they could begin anew during the next seven-year cycle.

Why does Leviticus move from the world of sacrifices to that of economic and social welfare? What could the Jewish people have been thinking as they received these mitzvot of the Sabbatical year and the treatment of the poor? They had never even seen their land, much less owned any of it. Rashi asks, "What is the relevance of being told of the Sabbatical year at Mount Sinai?" It would be years and years before the Jewish people would come in to the land, conquer it, and divide it up into the appropriate tribal sections. Even then, there would be an additional seven years before they could fulfill the commandment of resting during the Sabbatical year! Why did they need to learn about this commandment precisely at this moment in their incipient history?

Furthermore, the theme of the Sabbatical year had been previously introduced in the *parsha* of *Mishpatim* in the book of Exodus (23:11). Why were these laws not included there? Why do the laws of the Sabbatical and Jubilee years recur at this critical juncture, in the concluding messages of the book of Leviticus?

For twenty-four chapters, the Jewish people have been exhorted to become a holy people. Now, at the conclusion of the book of Leviticus, the two themes of *Behar* represent the true tests of the spiritual development of the Jewish people:

1. Will they have the spiritual strength not to work the land during the sabbatical year?
2. Will they have mercy and care for the poor, their powerless brethren?

Taken together, these two themes offer new hope for their society. The Jewish people have just fled from Egypt, where the strong enslaved the weak, the rich exploited the poor. This was their only model of social existence. Now they are being told that their society must be different and that there will always be hope for the less fortunate. No one will forever be financially burdened; within each person's lifetime his or her debts will be annulled and their land will be returned. No one will be abandoned; the treatment of the poor would become the focus of Jewish spirituality.

Economic and social laws do not form the core of the book of Leviticus, which concentrates on the centrality of the Tabernacle and the role of the priests and sacrifices in maintaining the holiness of the Jewish encampment. By choosing to close with these two themes, national holiness has transitioned into economic and social concerns.

HEARING YOUR OWN VOICE

1. How do you think that returning land and annulling debts during the seventh year would affect the economic structure of the society?
2. It was customary that during the Sabbatical year, the farmers would go to Jerusalem to study Torah. Are there any modern equivalents to this in your society?
3. What would you most want to do if you were to be given a Sabbatical year?
4. *Ayeka?* How can you recharge yourself now?

Shabbat Lunch

Deceitful Words

Is one allowed to window-shop? Am I allowed to walk into a store and ask the price of an item, if I have no intention of buying it?

This week's *parsha* states, "You should not defraud another, but you will fear your God, for I am the Lord your God" (Leviticus 25:17). Earlier in this *parsha*, the Torah already warned against financial fraud: "If you sell an object to your neighbor, or buy from him, you will not defraud one another" (Leviticus 25:14). What kind of fraudulent acts might have been excluded by the first commandment? What types of fraud does the second prohibition include?

The Mishnah states that "just as there may be deceit in monetary matters, so too, there may be deceit in verbal discourse. A person should not say [to a shopkeeper], 'How much does this item cost' if he has no intention of buying it. If a person has changed his life for the better, one should not say to him, 'remember your earlier actions'" (*Bava Metziah* 58b). The Talmud adds, "If one became ill or suffered family tragedies, don't talk to him the way that the friends of Job spoke to him, saying, 'Recall, now, was there ever someone that was innocent who perished?' (Job 4:7). If donkey drivers ask for grain, one should not send them to someone's home if one knows that he does not have any grain to sell [in order to embarrass that person]." Even calling someone by a derogatory nickname to which the person has become accustomed constitutes a form of verbal fraud, according to Jewish law, even if the person does not object to being called by the name.

What is the common denominator of these examples? What separates this type of speech from *lashon hara*?

These cases carry with them a trace of falseness and deception. If confronted, the speaker could always claim that his intentions were positive and pure – that is, he could claim that he really did intend to buy the object or that he really did think that there was grain at the home to which he sent the donkey drivers. In its most severe form, this type of verbal deceit can be acutely damaging, as, unlike cases of gossip, direct slander, or defamation, here the injured party has no potential recourse. The speaker can always claim, "I intended no harm, I meant well."

The Talmud posits that verbal deceit is more severe than monetary deceit, as the latter is possible to repay, while there is no way of alleviating the pain caused by deceitful words. Furthermore, while personal profit may provoke one to financially deceive another, there is no such incentive in cases of verbal damage and deceit; there is no benefit to be accrued, the speaker acts purely out of ill will.

This section of the Talmud concludes: "Since the time of the destruction of the Temple, the gates of prayer have been locked.... But even though the gates of prayer are locked, the gates of tears have not been locked.... Rav Hisda said, 'All of the gates are locked, except for the gates of those hurt by deception.'" The rabbis said that words and feelings that sincerely emanate from the heart have the power to enter the heart of another. So too the pain that is caused through subtle and guileful words can break a heart and has the power to break through the "locked gates of heaven."

HEARING YOUR OWN VOICE

1. If a person asks the price of an item with no intention of buying it, he has falsely raised the hopes of the shopkeeper. Can you think of additional reasons why this practice should be forbidden? Can you think of ways to overcome this problem?
2. What ramifications do you think that verbal deception may have for the field of advertising?
3. The Talmud states (*Bava Metzia* 58b) that the "placing of one's

eyes" on merchandise if one does not have the money to purchase it is also a form of fraud. Yet in this case, there is no other party involved. How do you understand this form of deception? What are the implications of this for the popular pastime of window-shopping?

4. *Ayeka?* Have you ever been tempted to buy something that you didn't need – or even want? What do you do to resist temptation?

Seuda Shlishit

The *Tzaddiks*' Response

"You should not defraud another, but you will fear your God, for I am the Lord your God" (Leviticus 25:17). In this *parsha*, the Torah cautions against the use of deceitful words (see "Behar/*Bechukkotai*: Deceitful Words"). What might be a person's response to having been misled?

Two leading rabbinical figures were, perhaps, unusual in their reactions to verbal deception.

The Rebbe from Szanz, noted for his giving of *tzedakah*, was once misled by the father of a bride. It once happened that the father of a bride came to ask the Szanzer Rebbe for money. In his community, it was customary for the bride's father to buy two *tallitot* (prayer shawls) for the prospective groom, one for the weekdays and one for Shabbat. The father told the rebbe that he did not have enough money to buy the *tallitot*. The rebbe prepared to give the father the necessary funds.

Suddenly, the elder son of the rebbe cried out, "Abba, the man is a liar! I saw him in the store just yesterday buying two *tallitot*!" The man turned pale and raced out of the rebbe's room.

The rebbe put his head in his hands and moaned, "*Oy vey, oy vey!* How could my son have done such a thing? Oy!" The rebbe leaned over and spoke very softly to his son. "Son, do you know what you have done? This man has a lot of expenses for the wedding. He simply thought that I would be more sympathetic to a request for money for something ritual, something sacred, than for other things. That is why he asked for money for the *tallitot*. Now, quickly run after him and bring him back here."

It is told that the Rebbe from Szanz did not forgive his son until he (the son) had helped to raise money for the whole wedding.

The Rebbe from Salant was once misled by a poor man shortly before Passover. The poor man asked him, "If I do not have enough money to buy wine, can I fulfill the obligation of seder night by drinking four cups of milk? "The rebbe replied that one cannot fulfill the mitzvah of the four cups by drinking milk, and then gave the poor man an extremely large amount of *tzedakah*.

When asked why he had given the man so much money, the rebbe replied, "You see, he wasn't only asking about the wine. Through his question (by asking specifically about milk), he was hinting to me that he also did not have enough money to buy meat for the Seder. I gave him money for both wine and meat."

HEARING YOUR OWN VOICE

1. How are these two cases different from other forms of verbal deception?
2. Martin Buber once said that it is not hard to answer the question that was asked, but it is very difficult to answer the question that was not asked. What do you think gave these rebbes the perception to answer the questions that were not asked? Do you know anyone else who has this quality?
3. When did you last respond to a question that someone was too embarrassed to ask? Did someone ever do this for you?
4. *Ayeka?* What advice would you give someone who wanted to become a better listener?

Numbers

Bamidbar:
Final Preparations

General Introduction to
the Book of *Bamidbar*

The fourth book of the Torah, *Bamidbar*, spans the forty years of the wanderings of the Jewish people in the desert. It chronicles their journeys from Mount Sinai to the plains of Mo'ab, which border the land of Israel. Unlike the two books of the Torah that immediately precede it, few commandments are given to the Jewish people in *Bamidbar*; rather, this book focuses on the crises, failures, and successes of the Jewish people during their wanderings in the desert and the lessons they learned from them.

In Genesis, Abraham is chosen, his mission is determined, and the twelve sons of Jacob become the prototypes of the twelve tribes of the nation. In Exodus, the Jewish people emerge and are given the Torah at Mount Sinai. In Leviticus, the laws concerning holiness, whether regarding the priests and the Tabernacle or involving general interpersonal relations, are transmitted. Now, the Jewish people are finally ready to begin their travels as a nation. Unlike when they departed from Egypt, they are now equipped with both their religious guidelines – the Ten Commandments – and their social and holy center, the Tabernacle.

The numerous incidents recounted in *Bamidbar*, such as the people's complaints for meat and water, the spies' fear of entering the Promised Land, the rebellion of *Korach* and his cohorts against Moses, and the cursing of the Jewish people by Bila'am are ostensibly one-time events in the history of the Jewish people. They are unique predicaments brought about by this singular period in history. The Jewish people will never again leave Egypt to travel to the Promised Land; the Jewish people will never again wander in a desert.

Why is there a need, then, to eternalize these seemingly one-time events into a book of the Torah? Why must they be remembered for all of time?

Each event in the book of Numbers epitomizes a situation that is destined to take place in each and every generation of the Jewish people. The crises that are recorded here are not "one-time" events; rather, they constitute prototypes that recur continually throughout Jewish history. Countless events must have occurred to the Jewish people during their forty years of wandering; however, only those that will revisit the Jewish people in the future are recorded in this book.

This week's *parsha*:

The first subject of this week's *parsha* is the counting of the Jewish people. Unlike the previous census, taken in the *parsha Ki Tissa* (Exodus 30:12), in which the Jewish people were counted as individuals upon contributing half a shekel to the building of the Tabernacle, now they are counted according to their respective tribes, in other words, "The numbering of the tribe of Reuben, 46,500.... The numbering of the tribe of Simeon, 59,300" (Numbers 1:21, 23). Furthermore, here the Torah states, "Take the sum of all the congregation of the children of Israel ... from twenty years old and upward, *all that are able to go forth to war* in Israel" (Numbers 1:2–3).

The second subject is the arrangement of the camp of the Jewish people into three concentric circles. At the innermost circle was the Tabernacle and its service, known as the "camp of the *Shechinah*" (the Holy Presence). The next circle, surrounding the Tabernacle, was divided into four regions, three populated by the Levites (*levi'im*) and one by the priests (*kohanim*). This circle was called "the camp of the Levites." This camp was devoted primarily to the care of the Tabernacle and matters of holiness. The remaining twelve tribes – Joseph received a double portion, as his tribe was divided between Efraim and Menashe – were organized into four groups of three, surrounding the camp, comprising what would be referred to as "the camp of Israel." In short, three very carefully structured circles of tribes formed the shape of the Jewish society.

Why does the book of *Bamidbar* begin with these procedures? Why were the counting of the Jewish people according to their tribes and the arrangement of the tribes into a well-organized system the first two events in the book of *Bamidbar*?

Before beginning their travels to the Promised Land, the Jewish people had to learn that they were not traveling as a mass of individuals but as a carefully orchestrated collective whole, with every person linked and responsible both to his or her community (tribe) and to the whole Jewish community. The Jews were not being counted as individuals but rather as potential soldiers preparing to serve in defense of the whole Jewish people.

The book of *Bamidbar* depicts the drama of a people in transition from slavery to freedom, from dependence to self-reliance. The Jewish people are now beginning to find their own way, both physically and spiritually, as a nation. This week's *parsha* outlines the final preparations before commencing this journey. The sanctuary is positioned at the people's center, the community alliances are publicly proclaimed, and the awareness of risking one's life for the sake of the entire nation is affirmed.

HEARING YOUR OWN VOICE

1. King David ordered the counting of the Jewish people (2 Samuel, chapter 24), and then regretted his action, referring to it as a great sin. Is there any danger inherent in counting people? Have you ever been "counted" as part of something? How did it make you feel?

2. The Jewish people no longer have a Tabernacle or sanctuary at their center. What do you think is the focal point of the Jewish people, of your own society? What would you like to be at its center?

3. In this *parsha*, the counting of the Jewish people and the arrangement of their camp is intended to foster a sense of national identity. How does one learn to think of one's own identity in national terms? How central is national identity in your life?

4. *Ayeka?* If you were given five minutes to talk to the Jewish People, what would you say?

Shabbat Lunch

Adolescent Growth

In Hebrew, the most holy name of God has four letters – *yud*, *heh*, *vav*, and a second *heh*. These four letters, together with the very first point of the first letter, represent five units that correspond to the five books of the Torah. Though the very first point of the first letter, the point at which the quill touches the parchment, is virtually imperceptible, it directs the path for the continuation of the writing. Symbolically, this infinitesimal point represents the moment of conception. It determines all future development. This first point corresponds to the first book of the Torah, Genesis, which, like the embryonic process, holds within it the concealed raw material and potential for all impending growth.

The first letter of God's name, *yud*, the smallest of all the letters, dangles unsupported in the air. It symbolizes birth and the beginning of actual life, the nascent stages of being. This *yud* corresponds to the second book of the Torah, Exodus, in which the Jewish people are born and precariously begin their first stages of life.

The second letter of God's name, *heh*, reflects the continuous growth and expansion of this birth process. This letter corresponds to the third book of the Torah, Leviticus, in which the Jewish people establish their camp and build the Tabernacle.

The first point of writing, together with the first two letters of God's name, compose a single unit denoting conception, birth, and growth. This reflects the process occurring in the first three books of the Torah.

The third letter of God's name, *vav*, corresponds to the fourth book of the Torah – Numbers, or *Bamidbar*. This letter, written as a straight vertical line, symbolizes an arrow pointing directly downward, toward the earth. The *vav* represents the transition from a "heavenly" existence to actual life in this "earthly" world. During the first three books of the Torah, the Jewish people were continually guided by "heavenly" direction. God chose Abraham, brought the Jewish people out of Egypt, and gave them the Ten Commandments. This chain of events set the stage for the Jewish people to act in this world, and now, in *Bamidbar*, they embark on their struggle to actualize their latent potential.

The book of *Bamidbar* thus represents the adolescence and young adulthood of the Jewish people, their movement from the supervision and parental care of childhood to the responsibility and independence of adulthood. This process is fraught with hazards, instability, and not a small number of crises.

The frame of mind necessary for this transition from dependence to independence is summarized in an expression in a Mishnah that describes the educational and spiritual guidance necessary for each stage of life, from the age of five to one hundred (*Pirkei Avot* 5:25). The period from twenty to thirty is designated as the time *"to pursue."* The transition from dependence – from fulfilling the directives of a higher source, be it God or a parent – to independence and finding one's own way is full of "pursuit."

What does "to pursue" imply about this stage in life? Why are ten years necessary for this endeavor?

The road to independence is never straight or simple. The Jewish people wandered in the desert, struggling with issues of authority, rebellion, jealousy, and fear. The many years that the Mishnah allocates to this process of self-discovery reflect the depth and complexity of this passage to maturity. To achieve independence, a person must be willing to explore and probe countless alternatives. "Pursuit" entails questioning, challenging, dreaming, and examining new ways of living and thinking. Through this process one begins to crystallize a personal outlook on life, cast in the uniqueness of his or her own personality and experience. The goal of this process is not simply to be unique but to be authentic; to fully believe in one's life rather than to live a life of imitation, mere acceptance, or fear of the unknown.

For the Jewish people, this process commenced with forty years of wandering in the desert. The divine and parental hand of God gradually withdrew and the Jewish people were left to learn from their mistakes and to forge their own identity. On the path to independence, only by making earthly mistakes and struggles can we strive for heavenly perfection and guidance.

HEARING YOUR OWN VOICE

1. The Talmud explains that one of the unique qualities of a desert is that it is utterly devoid of personal ownership or control. How else would you describe the uniqueness of the desert and what

its effect might be upon a people? Have you ever spent time in a desert, in the Sinai? How did it affect you?

2. The Mishnah, which describes the years from twenty to thirty as the time of "pursuit," describes the years from thirty to forty as the time of "strength (or power)." What qualities do you think this exemplifies?

3. What do you think happens to a person who never "pursues"? What characterizes your decade of "pursuit"?

4. *Ayeka?* When you look back at your growth toward greater independence and personal authenticity, what moment stands out for you as especially significant?

Seuda Shlishit

Old and New Flags

Every one of the children of Israel will camp with his own flag, with the insignias of their father's house.... (Numbers 2:2)

As they camped in the desert, each tribe of the Jewish people was marked by its flag. The unique color and design of each flag denoted the individual attributes and role that the tribe was supposed to play within the nation. With the emergence of the Zionist movement, the quest for a modern flag for the State of Israel began. Though today the Israeli flag is one of the most well-known symbols of the State, over one hundred years ago, neither its colors nor design had been determined.

Theodore Herzl recorded his idea for the flag in his diary: "Perhaps a white flag with seven golden stars. The white background would represent our new and pure life; the stars would represent the number of daily hours one would work in our society." Herzl approached Baron Hirsch, one of the leading Jewish benefactors of his time, with the initial thoughts of his plan, but it was never accepted. Other designs, including a Lion of Judah or a golden Star of David were also suggested, though none achieved significant popularity.

The source of today's blue and white flag came from David Wolffsohn (1856–1914), Herzl's associate and companion, who became the second president of the World Zionist Organization. Wolffsohn writes, "This matter (the design of the flag) caused me considerable distress. Suddenly, an idea popped into my head and everything became clear. In fact, we already had a flag – the 'tallit,' whose colors were white and dark blue.... I instructed that a white flag with two dark blue stripes and a *Magen David* (Star of David) in its center be made. It was immediately accepted as the national flag."

Numerous theories abound as to the meaning of the colors and the *Magen David* of the flag. Dark blue (in Hebrew, *tchelet*), the color originally intended for the *Magen David*, symbolizes the shade of water on the horizon, where it seems to blend into the sky. This signifies the uniting of the earthly and heavenly domains (Talmud, *Menachot* 43b). The two intertwining triangles composing the *Magen David* may represent the weaving together of the three sections of the Bible – Torah, Prophets, and Writings – with the three stages of time: past, present and future.

In addition to the significance of its design, Rabbi Joseph Soloveitchik writes that since its acceptance, the flag has assumed a new level of holiness. He writes that according to Jewish Law, a Jew who was killed in an act of anti-Semitism is buried in his or her bloodied clothes because the clothes acquire an element of sanctity through the blood that was spilled on them and also deserve a proper burial. All the more so, he writes, the flag of the State of Israel has acquired a spark of holiness by virtue of the thousands of Jews who have fallen in its defense. Honoring the flag of Israel is a sign of respect for their self-sacrifice.

HEARING YOUR OWN VOICE

1. What do you think the six points and the two triangles of the *Magen David* might represent?

2. Today, the stripes of the flag of Israel are not *tchelet* (dark blue) but rather a lighter shade of blue. At the inception of the state, the flag-makers had difficulty creating a dark blue dye that would not fade in the strong sun of the Middle East. A lighter, more durable, shade was therefore adopted. Suggestions have been made to return to the original dark blue shade and/or to add a Lion of Judah to it. What do you think?

3. What would you have suggested as the symbols of the flag of Israel? What spontaneously comes into your mind whenever you see the flag?

4. *Ayeka?* If you created a personal or family flag, what would it look like?

Naso

Parts of the Whole

In Genesis, Abraham was told, "and you will be a blessing" (Genesis 12:2). Abraham acquires the power to bless people's lives, to help them unite the physical and spiritual domains, to transform their awareness of the world. Now, six generations later, God's promise to Abraham is finally being fulfilled. This gift, in the form of the Priestly Blessing, is conveyed to Moses and Aaron:

> "May the Lord bless you and keep you;
> May the Lord make His face shine upon you, and be gracious to you;
> May the Lord lift up His face to you, and grant you peace."
> (Numbers 6:24–26)

Everything seems to be in place for the Jewish people to begin their mission. In last week's *parsha*, the organization of the camps of Israel was precisely defined. In this week's reading, the Jewish people have been endowed with the power to affect and elevate the world through their conduct, culminating with the Priestly Blessing. In next week's *parsha*, the Jewish people will finally depart from Mount Sinai and begin their journeys as an autonomous people. Yet one last piece is missing. For some reason, immediately preceding the Priestly Blessing, this week's *parsha* dwells on a number of paradigms of socially problematic behavior: (1) one who has stolen from a convert, (2) the *Sotah*, a woman suspected of being unfaithful to her husband, (3) the Nazirite, one who has taken an oath not to cut his hair or drink wine or strong drink.

Why are these cases mentioned before the Jewish people are ready for their mission? Is it by chance? Why has the Torah chosen this moment to discuss these problems?

An important principle is conveyed through the presentation and placement of these cases. Their presence illustrates that even with God's providential care in the desert, even with the wisdom of the Torah and leaders like Moses, Aaron, and Miriam, every human society is fraught with vices and failings. There will always be problems. There can be no blessing, no potential to perfect the world, if Jewish society has not first healed itself. Jewish society is not measured through external excellence and achievements but by its morality and its compassion for those who have, for whatever reason, stumbled morally. The value and well-being of Jewish society is determined by how well it facilitates the return of these individuals into its mainstream. No one is superfluous.

On a different level, a number of Hasidic commentators see these cases representing classic human failings. The thief has been physically tempted and hurt the community. The *Sotah* has failed to remain emotionally faithful to her husband and has hurt the family unit. The Nazirite has moved to spiritual excess, presenting an extreme relationship between the human being and God. The physical, emotional, and spiritual drives are all capable of consuming and controlling an individual.

Despite their failings, and the damage or pain they consequently inflict on the community, family, and spiritual dimensions of Jewish society, they remain part of the Jewish people. Before the Jewish people are able to bless others, they must themselves become whole; they must care for the health and welfare of each member.

HEARING YOUR OWN VOICE

1. The Nazirite strove to live on a higher spiritual level, refraining from a number of human activities (drinking wine, cutting his hair, etc.) and thus separating himself from the rest of society. Some commentators regard this effort as praiseworthy, while others judge it negatively. What do you think? What would be a modern example of this behavior?
2. Which of these drives (physical, emotional, and spiritual) do you think is the most difficult to control and direct positively for the majority of people? For you?
3. What blessing would you give to the Jewish people?
4. *Ayeka?* "No one is superfluous." What portion of the Jewish people do you have the most difficulty including? What small step do you think you could take to become more inclusive?

Shabbat Lunch

Home Schooling

This week's *parsha* states that when the Levites reach the age of thirty they should begin to perform the service of the Tabernacle. Yet in next week's *parsha* the Torah states that they should begin their service from twenty-five years and upward. The Talmud (*Chullin* 24a) resolves this apparent contradiction by stating that the Levites started learning their trade at twenty-five and began to actually work at the age of thirty.

The formal education of the Levites began at the age of twenty-five. What is the ideal age to begin schooling in general?

The Talmud (*Bava Batra* 21a) relates four steps that led to the creation of the public school system in Judaism:

Rav Judah said in the name of Rav: "Truthfully, the name of that man, Joshua ben Gamla, should be blessed, for if not for him, then the learning of Torah would have been forgotten from all of Israel! *For at first*, if a child had a father, his father taught him, and if he had no father, then he did not learn at all.... *Then* they made a decree that teachers of children should be appointed in Jerusalem.... Even so, if a child had a father, then the father would take him up to Jerusalem and have him taught there, and if not, then he would not learn at all. *Therefore*, they ordained that teachers should be appointed in each region, and that boys should enter school at the age of sixteen or seventeen. They did so, and if the teacher punished them they would rebel and run away from school. *Finally*, Joshua ben Gamla came and ordered that teachers of young children should be appointed in each district and town, and that children should enter school at the age of six or seven."

Though Joshua ben Gamla is remembered favorably, it seems that his approach was accepted reluctantly by Judaism. Despite their seemingly limited chances for success, two other options were adopted beforehand and were discarded only after they had failed. Apparently, the rabbis were reluctant to have children between the critical ages of six to sixteen removed from their home atmosphere.

Why was the option of public schooling not desired by the rabbis? What drawbacks might they have been worried about? Why was the home considered to be the ideal educational setting?

First of all, the relationship between the parent and child is not contingent upon the child's understanding of the material; their bond began long before the child commenced learning and will continue afterward. Thus the whole learning process ideally transpires in an environment of love, support, and caring. Unlike teachers who most likely instruct the child for only one year, acquiring a limited perception of the child, parents have watched their child grow during his or her whole life, hopefully observing his or her unique qualities, idiosyncrasies, and needs.

Second, the goal of parent-child education differs from that of a teacher-student relationship. The goal of a classroom setting is to convey material. Students are tested on how well they have understood the content of the classes. There is a yearly syllabus and projects, often determined before the students enter the classroom. In contrast, home schooling can be geared to a child's individual needs and qualities. In home schooling, the goal is not to transmit a set amount of material within a limited period of time but to convey values and lessons of life, which may take years to impart. The parent educates the "being" of the child, transmitting a way of life, rather than the material of the yearly syllabus.

Finally, the classroom setting creates an environment of comparison and competition (see "*Bereshit:* Aggression"), often at the expense of individual expression. Teachers learn how to "control" a classroom, and the establishment of order and discipline are essential skills to master. Individual students who may learn in a slightly different fashion or pace may be labeled as "problematic" or "disruptive." Students may begin to perceive themselves as being either "gifted" or "slow." The parent-child education, precisely because it affords itself a longer scope of time, is more likely to be free from the problematic consequences of comparison, labeling, and the rigid structure endemic to the classroom.

Home schooling has the potential to create an environment in which a loving parent who understands the unique qualities, needs, and learning patterns of his or her child can bequeath an education of a lifetime. However, as noted by the Talmud almost two thousand years ago, this ideal vision is rarely realized. As a result, the creation of the formal public school safeguarded the future of the learning of Torah.

HEARING YOUR OWN VOICE

1. In light of the selection from the Talmud quoted previously, Judaism understands that a teacher should see him- or herself

as a surrogate parent. What ramifications might this approach have for the classroom setting?

2. Why do you think that home schooling broke down? What other differences are there between these two educational settings?

3. Did the classroom setting help or hinder your educational development? Has your education reflected any of the ideas expressed here? How do you hope to educate your children?

4. *Ayeka?* If you were to set up a school, what would be special about it? What would be its spiritual message?

Seuda Shlishit

A Twentieth Century *Nazir*

And the Lord spoke to Moses, saying, "Speak to the children of Israel and say to them, 'When either a man or woman will pronounce a special vow of a Nazir to separate themselves to the Lord, he shall abstain from wine and strong drink ... no razor shall come on his head ... and he shall be holy, and shall let the locks of the hair of his head grow.'" (Numbers 6:1–5)

The drinking of wine and other strong drink is considered to be a primary form of social interaction; refraining from cutting one's hair is regarded as an antisocial act. The vows of the *Nazir* (Nazirite) served to distance the *Nazir* from society and, it is hoped, bring him or her to a new and higher level of spirituality. During the Temple period one could assume Nazirite vows for a limited or extended period of time. After the destruction of the Second Temple (70 CE), the observance of the Nazirite lifestyle appears to have disappeared, and for centuries there has been no record of individuals becoming Nazirites.

Nevertheless, one of the most unusual and extraordinary figures of Jerusalem during this century was known universally simply as "the Nazir." Rav David HaKohen (1886–1972) – philosopher, mystic, teacher, and writer – was recognized in Jerusalem by his long beard and flowing locks of hair, a contemporary *Nazir*.

Born to a rabbinic family near Vilna, the Nazir studied with the leading rabbis of Europe during his adolescent years. He continued his academic studies at universities in Germany and Switzerland, preparing a doctorate on the philosophy of religion, heavily influenced by the ideas of the German philosopher Hermann Cohen. In 1916 he met Rabbi Abraham Isaac Kook and began a lifelong relationship as his friend and disciple. For thirty years, the Nazir collected and edited Rabbi Kook's writings, eventually producing his three-volume epic called *Lights of Holiness*. The Nazir's own work, *The Voice of Prophecy*, comparing Jewish and Greek attitudes toward spirituality, won the Maimon Prize for literature.

While in Switzerland during World War I, the Nazir began to lecture at the University of Basel, achieving great success and popularity. Fearful that these accomplishments might engender feelings of pride or conceit, he decided to accept vows of a *Nazir*. For the rest of his life, the Nazir did not cut his hair, or drink wine or other intoxicating liquor. He became a lifelong vegetarian, and each year, for the forty days prior to Yom Kippur, he would abstain from all non-holy conversation. Legends abound of his refraining from sleep while studying through the night.

The Nazir chose his path in the search for holiness and prophecy. Strikingly, his choices did not remove him from involvement with his contemporary society. He raised his son, Shear Yashuv HaKohen, as a *Nazir* until the age of Bar Mitzvah. While still a lifelong vegetarian, Shear Yashuv chose to end his Nazirite behavior at the age of sixteen, eventually becoming the rabbi of the Israeli Air Force and serving as the chief rabbi of Haifa. The Nazir's son-in-law, Rabbi Shlomo Goren, was the rabbi of the Israeli Army and then chief rabbi of Israel.

After the death of Rav Kook in 1935, for over thirty years, the

Nazir did not leave his room, studying and writing most of the day. During the Six-Day War, as soon as the Israeli army regained the area of the Kotel (Western Wall), his son-in-law, Army Chaplain Shlomo Goren, sent his jeep for the Nazir, who is reputed to have been the first nonmilitary figure to reach the Wall. In his book, General Motte Gur, the leader of the paratrooper force that captured the Old City, reports that the soldiers stood in awe and amazement as the long-haired, aged rabbi, the Nazir, clutched the stones of the Western Wall.

HEARING YOUR OWN VOICE

1. When the *Nazir* (of the Torah) finished the period of being a Nazirite, he or she brought a sin-offering sacrifice. The commentators are divided over whether the "sin" of the *Nazir* was his or her *initial decision* to refrain from these activities, or whether it was the decision to *end* the period of being a *Nazir* and return to normal life. What do you think?

2. How might one evaluate whether the manifestations of a spiritual drive are healthy and productive or peculiar and unbalanced? What would you suggest to someone who wanted to grow spiritually?

3. Do you know individuals who have developed their spiritual side while still maintaining an involvement in mainstream affairs of society?

4. *Ayeka?* What is one small step you could take to become more holy?

Behaalotokha

Grumbling, Again

After almost a year of experiencing life-changing revelations, receiving the Ten Commandments, organizing themselves into distinct social units, and growing into a people with collective guidelines and a national vision, the Jewish people depart from Mount Sinai.

How would they look back upon their experience at Mount Sinai? What were their feelings as they left Mount Sinai?

Nachmanides quotes a Midrash that "they left Mount Sinai in joy, like a child fleeing from school, exclaiming, 'lest (God) give us more commandments.'" They could not wait to leave. Their perspective of the whole experience had shrunk into seeing only the burden of the rules placed upon them. Now, at last, they had the chance to run away from school.

This attitude of grief and resentment quickly found expression: "And the people complained..." (Numbers 11:1). The Torah never discloses the substance of their grumbling. Apparently, the content is not central to their leaving. Rashi states, "They simply sought any pretense to grumble, in order to distance themselves from God." Regarding the unusual word used here by the Torah to denote their

266

complaining (*k'mittonanim*), Samson Raphael Hirsch comments, "The people were as if mourning over themselves. They looked on themselves as already dead, and mourned over their very selves!"

Momentarily, their flight from Mount Sinai and subsequent grumbling finds concrete expression in the Torah. "And the children of Israel also wept again, and said, 'Who will give us meat to eat? We remember the fish, which we ate freely in Egypt; the cucumbers, the melons, the leeks, the onions, and the garlic, but now our soul has dried away; we have nothing to look at except the *manna*'" (Numbers 11:4–6). Now Egypt, the land of slavery and persecution, evokes fond memories; the house of bondage is transformed into a home for which they nostalgically yearn.

Upon hearing the last round of complaints, Moses seems to break down. When the people had complained of lack of water and food immediately after their departure from Egypt (Exodus 15:24–16:10), Moses had interceded with God on their behalf. He had prayed for them and shown great compassion. But now, one year later, Moses' resolve seems to be broken:

> And Moses heard the people weeping throughout their families … and Moses said to the Lord, "*Why have You afflicted Your servant? Why have I not found favor in Your sight, that You place the burden of this people upon me? Did I conceive this people? Did I give birth to them?* … Should I have to carry them like a wet nurse carries a baby? …
>
> From where should I have meat to give to this whole people when they cry to me? … I am not able to bear this people alone; it is too heavy for me. And if You deal like this with me, please kill me … and let me not see my own wretchedness." (Numbers 11:10–15)

What happened to Moses? Why doesn't he intercede on behalf of the Jewish people? How can it be that one year ago he said, "Forgive their sin, and if not, please blot me out of Your book" (Exodus 32:32), but now he pleads with God to let him abandon the people?

Rav Soloveitchik explains that now, after the Jewish people's latest outburst, Moses' assessment of the needs of the people, and of his relationship to them, has radically changed. Initially Moses understood that the transformation of the mass of slaves into a holy people would be achieved through education and that his role was primarily that of a teacher. Moses deemed himself capable of this task, and indeed history has accorded him the appellation of "Moses Rabbenu" (our teacher). Now, however, Moses' language reflects his realization that more than they need a teacher, they need a parent. "Did I conceive this people? Did I give birth to them? ... Should I have to carry them like a wet nurse carries a baby?" This role is quite different.

Unlike the teacher, who primarily conveys information and deals with intellectual faculties, the parent must understand and nourish all of the qualities of the child's personality. The role of a parent involves endless caring and nurturing. While the teacher can retain his or her own identity, parents must suspend their own needs while raising a small child.

Moses accepted the responsibility to teach the Jewish people and felt himself worthy of this challenge. But after their continual outbursts, after their seeking pretenses in order to grumble, Moses realized that more than a teacher was needed; a parent was essential to enable the Jewish people to mature into a stable people. For this role, he doubted his capabilities.

God granted Moses' request. "And the Lord said to Moses, 'Gather to Me seventy men of the elders of Israel' ... and the Lord took of the spirit that was upon him, and gave it to the seventy elders" (Numbers 11:16, 25). No longer would Moses have to bear the Jewish people by himself.

HEARING YOUR OWN VOICE

1. What do you think Moses' admission of inadequacy says about him as a leader? How do you think that the appointment of the seventy elders affected Moses' position as the leader of the Jewish people?

2. "Running away from Mount Sinai" is considered to be an eternal metaphor. Why do you think responsibility is often shirked? Is it possible to overcome this feeling? If you had been amidst the Jewish people at Mount Sinai, is there any law in particular from which you would have wanted to run away?

3. Have your Jewish role models been more like teachers or parents? Which do you think you need more? Which has been more effective?

4. *Ayeka?* What part of Judaism do you run away from? Why?

Shabbat Lunch

The Most Humble

And the man, Moses, was very humble, more so than all the men that were on the face of the earth. (Numbers 12:31)

In one of its most sweeping statements, the Torah defines the uniqueness of Moses. Not just "humble," not just "very humble" – Moses was the "most humble human being," beyond the scope of all the rest of humanity.

The Torah never attributes such superlatives to Abraham, Isaac, or Jacob, or to Sarah, Rebecca, Leah, or Rachel. In fact, very rarely does the Torah ascribe qualities to any of its major figures (Noah and Jacob being notable exceptions). Furthermore, Moses has many character traits, yet this one alone is singled out.

Why does the Torah place such emphasis on this quality of Moses? What distinguishes the "humble" person?

Humility is often confused with meekness or timidity; the docile or obsequious personality may be mistakenly called humble. Yet throughout his period of leadership, Moses demonstrated assertiveness and courage. He stands up to Pharaoh, boldly breaks the tablets of the Ten Commandments, and continually resolves crises among the Jewish people. In what way, then, is Moses "humble"?

Humility is *not* continually deferring to other opinions or believing that one does not have special gifts; rather, humility is believing that one's special talents, are, in fact, gifts. Each person has been granted unique and special powers with which to effect positive change in this world. The humble person understands that he has been bestowed with these powers not for personal fulfillment but rather for influencing the world. Personal abilities are always accompanied with the requisite obligation and responsibility of using them productively. Unlike the self-centered personality who looks upon his or her achievements with a sense of personal accomplishment, the humble individual removes the "I," or the ego-fulfillment, from the centrality of the task at hand. There is a very subtle though poignant altering of subject and emphasis: it is not that *I* am performing these tasks, but rather *these tasks* need to be accomplished by me.

Ironically, humility is the primary quality necessary for successful leadership. Only a person who is not concerned with self-fulfillment can clearly perceive the intended objective. Only a person who does not confuse this greater vision with concerns of self-esteem can become an ideal leader. Moses did not seek out a leadership role. When Moses was originally approached by God to lead the Jewish people out of Egypt (Exodus, chapter 3), he declined, asserting that he was not suitable for the part. When God offered to destroy the Jewish people and to create a new people from Moses, he protested.

The Talmud (*Ta'anit* 7a) states that the quality of humility is essential for learning Torah. The learning of Torah should not be exploited to build up one's own reputation; rather, one should learn in order to fulfill the task of improving the world. Ultimately, the Talmud (*Shabbat* 89a) states that because Moses was humble and was not concerned with his own self-image, he was rewarded by having the Torah called *Torat Moshe*, the "The Torah of Moses."

HEARING YOUR OWN VOICE

1. Rav Kook writes that true humility strengthens one's resolve and is reflected in a growing sense of happiness; in contrast, despondency or despair reflect perversions of true humility. Why?
2. Do you know of any leaders today whom you would consider to be humble?
3. Have you struggled with feelings of pride over your personal achievements?
4. *Ayeka?* What advice would you give yourself to bring more humility to your work and life?

Seuda Shlishit

Education of a Child-Rebbe

From the age of twenty-five until fifty years old, the Levites tended to all matters of holiness in the Tabernacle and, eventually, in the Temple. Moses was ordered to "separate out the Levites from among the children of Israel; and the Levites shall be Mine [God's]" (Numbers 8:14).

It is not simple to raise a child to become a religious leader. The hasidim relate the following educational approach:

The rebbe was about to die. He had served his people well for a long time, and now he was prepared to move on to a better world. Before he died, he called together his closest disciples and carefully advised them how to raise the future rebbe, his son.

The rebbe passed away, and his son was proclaimed as the new rebbe. Though only a child, the new rebbe had already been recognized as a wondrous prodigy. People came from all over to ask him their most personal and difficult questions; his answers did not disappoint them. He tirelessly served his followers, soon becoming beloved by all those in the community.

Yet every afternoon, his father's closest disciples would mysteriously lead him to a place that no one ever discovered. Every afternoon, for several hours, the young rebbe's whereabouts were a mystery to all.

Legends abounded about the miracles that he wrought during these times. "Surely," claimed one of his followers, "he is traveling in the most holy of worlds." Another asserted with the greatest confidence, "He is praying for all those who are suffering. He doesn't want us to see his tears." They argued incessantly over his possible feats. Was he studying the secrets of the Kabbalah? Was he bringing the Messiah?

Years passed, and the child-rebbe became aged. He now realized that his time was approaching to be called to the heavenly court.

His faithful followers approached him one last time. "Rebbe," they hesitantly asked, "can you finally reveal to us where you went during those times when the advisers stole you away? What were you doing? All these years, we could never truly fathom your mysterious disappearance."

With benevolent love, the rebbe's eyes caressed his followers. "You must understand," he began, "that my father was the most wise of men, the most loving of fathers. He knew what my future held for me. Therefore, he carefully bade his advisers to carry me away and occupy me during every afternoon of my childhood. They would bring me to a room, and there, they would give me a box. What was in the box? Marbles. Every afternoon, my father wanted to be certain that I would play marbles."

HEARING YOUR OWN VOICE

1. Why do you think that the Rebbe instructed that his son play marbles?
2. In *Pirkei Avot* (Ethics of the Fathers 5:25) it is stated that children should begin to learn Torah at the age of five. Based upon this, the rabbis instruct that parents should not try to teach their children how to read before the age of five; rather, the early years should be safeguarded for experiential forms of education. What do you think?
3. What would be adult equivalents of playing marbles? What is yours?
4. *Ayeka?* How do you think spirituality could be taught? How would you teach spirituality to yourself?

Shelach Lecha

Generations of Crying

The Jewish people leave Mount Sinai; they are only a few days' journey from the Promised Land. Yet this generation will never enter the land. They will "wander in the wilderness for forty years.... According to the number of the days in which you spied out the land, forty days, each day for a year, you will bear your transgressions" (Numbers 14:33–34). Because of the sin of the spies, the entire generation is sentenced to wander for forty years, dying homeless in the desert.

What went wrong? What was the sin of the spies?

Twelve spies, the leaders of each of the tribes, were sent to examine the Promised Land. In the book of Deuteronomy, Moses relates that it was neither his nor God's idea to send spies to explore the land; rather, the people proposed the plan, and Moses acquiesced. "And you all came near to me [Moses] and said, 'We will send men before us, and they will search out the land, and bring us back word by what way we must go up, and into what cities we will come'" (Deuteronomy 1:22). After forty days, the spies brought back the following report: "We came to the land where you sent us, and indeed it flows with milk and honey; and this is the fruit of it. *But* (*effes*) the people are strong that dwell in the land, and the cities are fortified, and very great" (Numbers 13:27–28).

Was this purely a scouting report? In the account of the spies, which would become known in history as the "evil report," a single word ignominiously stands out: "but" (*effes*). Instead of objectively recounting their mission, the spies passed judgment that entering the land would be too great a challenge for the people. The spies continued: "[It is a] land that consumes its inhabitants, and all the people that we saw in it were men of great stature. There we saw the giants ... and we were like grasshoppers in our own eyes, and so too we were in their eyes." The spies, the leaders of the Jewish society, succeeded in breaking the hearts of the people, "and the people wept on that night" (Numbers 14:1).

What were these leaders of the Jewish people afraid of?

The *Zohar* states that the spies "were misled by a false reasoning. They said (to themselves): If the Jewish people enter the land, then we (the spies) will be superseded, since it is only in the wilderness that we are considered worthy to be leaders." The spies were afraid not of being defeated by "the men of great stature," but of losing their own stature within the community. The leaders sought to protect their individual fortunes and insidiously misled the people. They were concerned that the present social framework would change once the people entered the land, and they were troubled by the fact that their type of leadership was appropriate only for this particular time, for a people in transition.

According to the Talmud, not only did the generation of the Exodus suffer, but "God declared that 'since [in the desert] you cried for no valid reason, I swear that every future generation will also cry on this day'" (*Ta'anit* 29a). The day on which the spies returned with their evil report, the ninth of Av, was destined to become the most calamitous day in Jewish history. The Mishnah records five catastrophes that occurred on the ninth of Av, including the destruction of the First and Second Temples.

Whenever the leaders of the Jewish people place their self-interest before the national concerns, or whenever the leaders of the Jewish people regard themselves as insignificant, "we were like grasshoppers in our own eyes," then the echoes of the crying on that night still resound. Part of the lesson of the spies is knowing what is truly worthy to cry about.

HEARING YOUR OWN VOICE

1. Before the spies departed, Moses changed the name of one of the spies, Hoshea, meaning "one who *has* saved us," to Yehoshua (Joshua), meaning "one who *will* save us." Moses already had an inclination of the intentions of the spies and wanted to empower Joshua to withstand their machinations. Do you know anyone who has become empowered, or has better withstood the forces of social pressure, through changing his or her name?

2. How does one's self-perception affect one's behavior? What is the difference between seeing oneself as "small as a grasshopper" and being very humble?

3. The events of the generation of the desert are considered to be eternal paradigms, occurring in every community and generation in our history. Do you think that we have learned the lesson and overcome the failure of the spies, or are there still symptoms of this failure in our times?

4. *Ayeka?* "Crying for no valid reason." During the last year, did you ever cry or become despondent over something that now seems unwarranted?

Shabbat Lunch

Attitudes toward the Land of Israel

The sin and tragedy of the spies prevented the generation of the desert from entering the Land of Israel. For the last two thousand years, other obstacles, ranging from poverty and danger to ideological opposition to *aliyah* ("ascent," the Hebrew term for moving to Israel), have stood in the Jew's path to Israel. During the last century, many waves of *aliyah* have come to Israel, for many utterly distinct reasons and goals.

Theodor Herzl (see "*Vayakhel/Pekudei*: Building Dreams") called the Jews to return to Israel to evade the harsh anti-Semitism of Europe. Similarly, another early Zionist thinker, Leon Pinsker, wrote that the existence of the Jews as a nonassimilated, separate, ethnic entity in Europe would forever arouse the hatred of the nations. These Zionist thinkers sought a haven for the Jews, entertaining even the possibilities of Uganda and Argentina.

In 1904, at the age of forty-eight, A.D. Gordon came to Israel, where he worked as a manual laborer in the vineyards of Petach Tikvah, and then moved to the Galilee. Gordon began to formulate what would eventually be referred to as "the religion of labor." Asserting that the human's relationship to God had become severed through the detachment from nature, Gordon called for an almost mystical rejuvenation of the soul through physical labor and connection to the soil. This bond to nature would enable the people to rediscover their spirituality and to regain a sense of cosmic unity and holiness.

A different kind of Zionism was advocated by rabbis who supported *aliyah* because it would enable the fulfilling of particular mitzvot that were impossible to observe while living outside of

Israel. These include tithing the produce of the land and refraining from working the land during the Sabbatical year. The first chief rabbi of pre-State Israel, Abraham Isaac Kook, combined the idea of the mystical holiness of the land and their respective mitzvot. He wrote that the holiness of the land did not simply enable the Jews to perform a few more mitzvot, but transformed all the mitzvot and all of their lives. Its effect upon the Jewish people was something that was impossible for one's cognitive powers to fully appreciate. "The Land of Israel is not something external, not an external national asset, or a 'means' to create collective solidarity ... [rather it] is an essential constituent bound to the life-force of the people" (*Orot*). Just as a flower can only thrive in its proper soil, so too the thought, life, and action of the Jewish people can only truly flourish in the Land of Israel. The development of this national awareness is necessary to bring about the salvation of the world.

HEARING YOUR OWN VOICE

1. In 1889, Ahad Ha'am (pseudonym of Asher Hirsch Ginsberg) wrote "The Wrong Way," in which he vigorously criticized the early Zionist movement for placing a premature emphasis on settlement in Israel. Ahad Ha'am advocated that more cultural and educational work be done outside of Israel, as a precursor to mass *aliyah*. What do you think are the most significant cultural or educational achievements presently occurring outside of Israel? In Israel?

2. What do you think has been the effect of the return to Israel on the Jewish people as a whole? What challenges do you think it presents for the State of Israel?

3. With which of the approaches to *aliyah* discussed in this unit do you most identify?

4. *Ayeka?* Why do you think the Torah places such a central value

on the national aspect of Judaism? What holds you back from being more connected to the Jewish people?

Seuda Shlishit

Fruits of Paradise

Moses instructed the spies to explore the land of Israel. He told them to check "whether the land is fat or lean, whether there are trees in it or not . . . and bring back the fruit of the land" (Numbers 13:20). The spies returned with pomegranates, figs, and clusters of grapes. They showed the fruit to the people and told Moses, "We came to the land where you sent us, and indeed it flows with milk and honey, and this is the fruit of it" (Numbers 13:27). The bounty of the fruit of the Land of Israel was an indicator of its being blessed.

During Talmudic times, when faced with a choice of eating fruit grown in Israel or in the Diaspora, many rabbis favored eating those indigenous to the land. A legend relates that the *Orach Chayim*, a leading Jerusalem rabbi, would only eat produce grown in Israel.

Is there something unique about the fruit that grows in Israel and draws its nourishment from the land? Certainly, countries all over the world produce delicious-tasting fruit. What is special about something that has grown in *Eretz Yisrael*?

The Talmud relates the remarkable qualities of one particular fruit of Israel, "the fruit of *Ginosar*," grown near the lake of Galilee.

> Rabba Bar Bar Chana recounted: "One time we accompanied Rabbi Yochanan to eat the fruit of *Ginosar*. If there were one hundred of us, each one of us would give him ten pieces of fruit. If there were ten of us, each one would bring him one hundred pieces. Each bundle of one hundred pieces would fill up a basket of almost one hundred pounds of fruit. Rabbi Yochanon

would eat all of them (!), and then swear to us that it was as if he had not eaten anything, that he was not yet full.... Rabbi Shimon Ben Lakish would eat them until he became dazed [confused and bewildered]. (*Berakhot* 44a)

The fruit of *Ginosar* had such wonderful qualities that the rabbis stated that it was good that it did not grow in Jerusalem, for if it did, people would come up to Jerusalem in order to eat its fruit, rather than to experience the city itself.

No one knows exactly what was so special about this particular fruit. The Midrash, however, proposes a theory, based on its name. *Ginosar* may be the conjunction of two words: *Gan* (garden) and *Sar* ("prince" or "guardian angel"). The fruit of *Ginosar* was the yield of a royal, perhaps heavenly, garden. One could eat it without becoming full, like Rabbi Yochanan. On the other hand, it had the power to cause someone to lose touch with this world, like Rabbi Shimon Ben Lakish.

Thus the fruit of this heavenly garden, like the fruit of the original Garden of Eden, could be both special and perilous at the same time.

HEARING YOUR OWN VOICE

1. The rabbis of the Talmud (*Berakhot* 40a) speculate and disagree over the type of fruit that was on the "Tree of Knowledge of Good and Evil" in the Garden of Eden. A number of theories are offered regarding the fruit that was the original cause of sin; a grapevine, fig tree, and wheat (!) are offered as possibilities. In what way could each of these fruit be seen as responsible for sin?

2. According to Jewish mystical sources, each piece of fruit carries within it a force of life, a soul, and the fruit grown in the Land of Israel is considered to have an additional level of holiness. When one eats and becomes nourished by this fruit,

one absorbs the vitality of the Land. The Mishnah focuses on a play on words and states that the "fruit" that one eats ultimately influences the "fruit" of one's labors. Has your behavior ever been influenced spiritually by the types of fruits (or food) that you eat?

3. What fruit do you think would be most similar to the "fruit of *Ginosar*" today?

4. *Ayeka?* Do you feel there is a spiritual aspect to your eating? What is one small step you could take to make eating a more spiritual experience?

Korach

Rebellion

Korach, Moses' cousin, fomented the first rebellion in Jewish history. Together with his group of followers, he harshly and directly attacked the leadership of Moses and Aaron. The Mishnah states that Korach and his group epitomize an unholy alliance united for personal gain, and he is condemned in rabbinic writings for having acted from impure motives. "What controversy was not in the Name of Heaven [for righteous ends]? The controversy of Korach and all of his company" (*Ethics of the Fathers* 5:20).

What was Korach's complaint?

> Now Korach, the son of Yitzhar, the son of Kehat, the son of Levi, and Datan and Aviram … took men. And they rose up before Moses, together with two hundred and fifty leaders of the community, men of renown. They gathered themselves together against Moses and against Aaron, and said to them, "You take too much upon yourselves. All of the congregation is holy, every one of them, and the Lord is among them, why do you raise yourselves up above the congregation of the Lord?" (Numbers 16:1–3)

At first glance, it seems that Korach's complaint is quite legitimate. Isn't, in fact, the whole congregation holy? Didn't the Torah state at Mount Sinai, "And you shall be to Me a kingdom of Priests and a *holy nation*?" (Exodus 19:6). Isn't Korach simply being a leader of the people, standing up for them and defending their rights? Why does Moses immediately distrust Korach's motivation?

Three signs alert Moses to the true nature of Korach's intentions. First, Korach's personal background leading up to his allegations. Why does Korach protest against Moses and Aaron precisely now, rather than during the first year of their leadership? According to the Midrash, Korach had a personal reason for inciting the rebellion now:

> What induced Korach to quarrel with Moses? He was envious of the position bestowed upon Elitzaphan, the son of Uziel, whom Moses had appointed to be prince over the sons of Kehat. Korach argued: "My father and his brothers were four in number: Amram, Yitzhar, Hevron and Uziel. The two eldest sons of the first-born son, Amram, [Moses and Aaron], have assumed important positions; thus who should be entitled to receive the second level of ranking if not myself, since I am the son of Yitzhar, who was the second-born? Yet, who has been appointed as prince of the tribe, if not the son of the fourth-born and youngest brother, Uziel?! (Numbers 3:30). I hereby protest against him [Moses] and will undo his decision."

Second, the masses of people aligned with Korach aroused Moses' suspicions. Some protested against the positions of leadership assumed by Moses and Aaron, "You take too much upon yourselves"; others griped over the lack of success of their leadership: "Is it a small thing that you have brought us up out of a land flowing with milk and honey (!), to kill us in the wilderness" (Numbers 16:13). In a classic example of demagoguery, Korach banded together an array of malcontents, each burning with his own issue.

Their particular issues became secondary to launching a frontal attack on Moses and Aaron.

Third, the style of Korach and his assembly was excessively brusque and contemptuous of Moses and Aaron. Two of Korach's co-conspirators, Datan and Aviram, refused to meet with Moses. "And Moses sent for Datan and Aviram ... and they said, 'We will not come up'" (Numbers 16:12). They were not interested in engaging in a discussion with Moses, but in lowering his standing in the eyes of the community.

As discussed earlier (see "*Shelach*: Generations of Crying"), the crises of the generation of the desert are considered to be inherent in every generation. Unlike the spies who wanted to *maintain* their personal standing within the community, Korach and his assembly sought to *advance* their communal status and power. The test of Moses as a national leader was to discern the merit and integrity of his challengers. Ultimately, Korach, who craved to raise his status, was plunged into an endless descent when the earth opened its mouth and swallowed him alive. "They, and everything they owned, went down alive to She'ol, and the earth closed upon them and they perished from among the congregation" (Numbers 16:33). Just as Datan and Aviram had unwittingly predicted, Moses' challengers did not "go up"; rather, they descended forever.

HEARING YOUR OWN VOICE

1. Which of the three factors mentioned previously (the background, alignment, and style) is the most characteristic of disingenuous political protests and movements?

2. Some commentators maintain that Korach wanted to eliminate the hierarchy within the Jewish people and to establish a populist ruling body. If so, should Moses have resisted this initiative? What are the advantages and disadvantages of a hierarchical political system?

3. Is there "a voice of Korach" within each person? The author of one of the earliest Hasidic writings, the *Tanya*, states that it is almost impossible to perform an act of pure giving, without any intention of receiving something in return. How is it possible to check whether one's behavior is wholly benevolent or mingled with personal concerns?

4. *Ayeka?* Have your protests ever been mingled with a personal agenda? How do you check your motivation?

Shabbat Lunch

The Afterlife

And it came to pass ... that the ground split beneath them [Korach and his followers]. The earth opened her mouth, and swallowed them up, and their houses, and all the men that were allied with Korach, and all their goods. They, and all that belonged to them, went down alive to She'ol [the nether world], and the earth closed upon them, and they perished from among the congregation. (Numbers 16:31–33)

Korach had impugned the authority of Moses and, together with all his family and followers, was swallowed alive. Yet the Torah mysteriously notes later, "The children of Korach did not die" (Numbers 26:11). The Talmud (*Sanhedrin* 110a) and its commentaries explain that the children of Korach descended with him to She'ol (purgatory), but because of their remorse over their actions, a special place was created for them there. Somewhere in the depths of She'ol, says the Talmud, they forever sing, "Moses and his Torah is true, and we are impostors."

How does Judaism understand what happens to someone after death?

Notwithstanding several references to this obscure region

She'ol, the Torah does not directly address the issue of life after death. Furthermore, there seems to be no consensus in the sources of what happens in the afterlife.

Some commentators, based on an allusion in the first book of Samuel (25:29), which describes the soul being "tossed about, as if from a slingshot (*kaf hakalah*)," understand that the first stage of life after death is characterized by perpetual affliction and agony of the soul. In this stage, the soul watches and reviews its life *again and again*, feeling increasing distress over moments wasted and decisions poorly made. The remorse felt over each unfulfilled moment of life serves as a "cleansing process" (*tikkun*) for the soul, which provides correction for the person's failures in this world. Until one feels complete regret over each nonactualized moment, the soul is forced to "toss and turn" without rest.

Though not mentioned in either biblical or talmudic sources, the Kabbalah described an intricate system of reincarnation (*gilgul neshamot*), in which the soul, after departing from one's body, would return to the physical world in succeeding generations. Rabbi Moshe Chaim Luzzatto, an eighteenth-century mystic and author, wrote that a soul would continually be united with a new body until it had fulfilled its destined purpose in this world; each new cycle would perfect flaws of a previous life. Luzzato wrote, though, that it is impossible for human beings to understand why or how this occurs. Nevertheless he considered himself (Moshe/ Moses) and his wife, Tzipporah, to be somehow the incarnations of the souls of their biblical namesake, Moses and Tzipporah.

Following a more rationalist approach, Maimonides wrote that one should not dwell on matters of the afterlife, because "concerning all of these things, a person will not understand them until they happen … they are not the essence of Judaism" (Laws of Judges 12:2). Similarly, the Maharal of Prague (1525–1609) wrote that the "The World to Come" is not mentioned in the Torah so that one will focus all efforts and attention to the perfection of this world.

The whereabouts of the children of Korach remain a mystery.

HEARING YOUR OWN VOICE

1. Which of the approaches mentioned above (Luzzato, Maimonides, or Maharal) appeals most to you? Why?
2. Did you ever know someone who had a near-death experience or "saw their life flash before their eyes"? How did it affect them?
3. Do you ever think about the afterlife? Does this affect or concern your present living?
4. *Ayeka?* How does your understanding of the afterlife affect your present living?

Seuda Shlishit

Leading Astray

Korach's pride caused him to lead himself and his followers astray. He exploited his position of leadership for personal gains.

Two hundred years ago, the Hasidic rabbi Ya'akov Yosef of Polonnoye (d. c. 1782) bitterly castigated the leaders of his generation for their egotistical behavior. One of the foremost students of the Ba'al Shem Tov and a major ideologue of the Hasidic movement, he caustically wrote of "two plagues" of his generation:

> Our souls are sick of listening to *hazzanim* (cantors), for in every fine and pious community the plague has spread. They sin and bring others to sin. When they prolong their melodies without end, the people gossip in the synagogue, interrupting the silence of prayer at times when it is forbidden to interrupt. Therefore the hazzan brings evil upon himself and upon others. Originally, I heard, he sang devoutly and without payment, for the hazzan was the most important person in the city.... But in the course of time, when the generation was no longer pure,

only the melody remained, while the hazzan ceased to pray at all.... Woe for the disgrace! How has he the shamelessness to stand up as the advocate, the messenger of the congregation...?

A plague has spread among the rabbis regarding the sermons they preach on the Sabbath before Passover and on the Sabbath of Repentance (the Shabbat before Yom Kippur). For the principal purpose of the sermon should be to show the people the path upon which they should tread.... But at the present time it is otherwise, for the rabbis use most of their sermons to display their brilliance and their knowledge, while toward the end they just mention a few laws regarding Passover and none at all on the Sabbath of Repentance. [*Toldot Ya'akov Yosej*]

HEARING YOUR OWN VOICE

1. Have you ever encountered examples of the "two plagues" that Rabbi Ya'akov Yosef spoke about? Have you encountered cantors or rabbis who did not exhibit these qualities? Who?
2. Rabbi Ya'akov Yosef did not seek to abolish positions of leadership, but rather to instill these positions with a new vitality. He wrote at length of the *tzaddik* (the holy or completely righteous leader), a figure who would serve as the connection between "the heavens and the earth," between God and the people, regarding all matters of life. The establishment of this position aroused the anger of the more conventional leaders, who feared that it would encourage an almost cult-like circle of followers. Have you ever met someone who you would consider to be a *tzaddik*? Do you share the concerns of those who opposed this institution?
3. Have you ever been in a position of leadership in which you struggled with feelings of vanity over your accomplishments?
4. *Ayeka?* What piece of advice would you give yourself to help reduce your drive for recognition and popularity?

Chukkat

Mysteries

The name of this week's *parsha*, *Chukkat*, comes from the term *chok*, which refers to decrees that reflect the mysterious and inexplicable ways of God. Unlike *mishpatim*, laws that the human being can potentially comprehend, *chukim*, by definition, remain beyond the scope of human comprehension and are utterly unfathomable.

The *parsha* begins with the preeminent example of a *chok*, the purification of a person who has become defiled (through contact with a dead body) by sprinkling the ashes of a red heifer over him or her. This *parsha* symbolizes that which is beyond human understanding; thus it comes as no surprise that its unifying theme is the reality and mystery of death.

In this week's *parsha*, the Torah jumps almost imperceptibly from the *second* year of the wandering of the Jewish people in the desert to the *fortieth*. The generation of the Exodus from Egypt, the generation that had cried over the evil report of the spies, has died. The deaths of Moses' sister, Miriam, and brother, Aaron, are also related in this week's *parsha*.

One of the most baffling and perplexing events of the *parsha* is

God's punishment of Moses – forbidding him to lead the Jewish people into the Promised Land.

After the death of Miriam, the Jewish people complained about their lack of water. God then tells Moses:

> Take the rod, and gather the assembly together, you, and Aaron your brother, and *speak* to the rock before their eyes; and it will give forth its water, and you will give the congregation and their beasts drink. And Moses took the rod from before the Lord, as He commanded him. And Moses and Aaron gathered the congregation together before the rock, and he said to them, "Hear now, *you rebels*; will *we* bring water out of this rock for you?" And Moses lifted up his hand, and *hit* the rock with his stick *two times*; and the water came out abundantly, and the congregation drank, and their beasts also.
>
> And the Lord spoke to Moses and Aaron, "Because you did not believe in Me, to sanctify Me in the eyes of the children of Israel, therefore you will not *bring* this congregation in to the land which I have given them." (Numbers 20:8–12)

What exactly was Moses' sin? What could have been so wrong that the faithful leader of the Jewish people for forty years would never finish his life's task of bringing the people into the land?

The exact nature of Moses is never revealed in the Torah. Numerous theories abound. According to Maimonides, Moses' sin was his outburst of anger in front of the whole congregation, calling them *"you rebels"* (Introduction to *Pirkei Avot*, chapter 4). Maimonides assumed that a leader of Moses' stature should have been able to control his frustration. Rashi writes that Moses was told to *"speak* to the rock," and by *hitting it* he reduced the profoundness of the moment. Nachmanides attributes the source of Moses' mistake to his hitting the rock *twice*, as if two different sources of the miracle were communicating with him.

Moses does not utter a word of protest upon receiving his punishment of not bringing the people into the land. The punishment appears to focus on the failure of leadership, since it implies that he no longer merits *bringing* the people into the land.

Forty years earlier, when the Jewish people complained over the lack of water in the desert (see "*Beshallach*: Growing Pains"), Moses was told to hit the rock to bring forth water (Exodus 17:1–7). Forty years later, Moses hears a similar complaint, yet now it arises from a different generation. Nevertheless, *he responds in exactly the same manner as before*: he hits the rock. Perhaps one of the qualities of leadership is knowing how to react differently to each situation, never relying upon earlier accomplishments, and Moses' response had not changed despite the elapsing of time and changing of the generation.

Notwithstanding the countless attempts to understand this moment in history, it appears that it will forever remain a *chok*, an eternal mystery, hidden both to the Jewish people and Moses.

HEARING YOUR OWN VOICE

1. Which of the various explanations of Moses' sin mentioned previously do you think is the most plausible? Why do you think that the Torah never disclosed the actual reason?
2. This week's *parsha* remains one of the most mysterious in all of the Torah. Why do you think that the Torah sets forth rules or experiences that are, by definition, beyond human understanding?
3. Despite receiving notification of this heartbreaking punishment, Moses continued to lead the people until his death. How have you grappled with your greatest disappointment?
4. *Ayeka?* How do you relate to the Torah's *chukim*, its nonrational laws? Does nonrational reasoning stand behind some, any, of your behaviors?

Shabbat Lunch

Anger

In this week's *parsha*, once again, the people complain about their life in the desert. Before Moses hits the rock, he reprimands them, saying, "Hear now, you rebels; from this rock shall we bring forth water for you?!" (Numbers 20:10). Moses, who had previously been described as the "most humble man on the face of the earth" (Numbers 12:3), seems to explode in anger. As discussed previously, according to several commentators, including Maimonides, it was because of this outburst that Moses was punished and not allowed to lead the Jewish people into the Promised Land.

Anger is sometimes provoked by seemingly insignificant annoyances or by feelings of wounded pride or self-respect. Yet neither of these explanations seems applicable to Moses. After selflessly guiding the people for almost forty years in the desert, why did Moses suddenly become so enraged?

The Talmud (*Ta'anit* 4a) explains that a person's yearning for truth and the improvement of the world can also lead to exasperation and short-temperedness. This anger is not a result of feelings of personal affront or injury; rather, it is motivated by a sense of frustration and despair over the increasing gap between an ideal world and the present reality. Leaders are especially subject to these feelings of disappointment. Maimonides writes that when community leaders perceive the need to reprove their constituents, they should *"show a face"* of anger, while never *actually* becoming angry. In order to effectively discipline the community, leaders should appear to be angry, they may assume a facade of harshness or severity, but they should remain calm and levelheaded within.

For a moment, Moses *actually* became angry. He lost perspective of the nature and the emotional make-up of the people and lost sight of what they needed and why they complained. For a moment, he did not focus on their needs but on his own pain, and he was overcome with his frustration at not having successfully raised the people beyond their immediate needs. Thus his anger was not educational, but personal.

The Torah, of course, never prohibits becoming angry. As seen from the fact that even Moses got angry, it is apparently an aspect of human nature that is impossible to completely sublimate or deny. Nevertheless, anger was considered to be self-indulgent and was strongly condemned by the rabbis of the Talmud and major Jewish thinkers.

The primary danger inherent in becoming angry is losing self-control. The Mishnah (*Pirkei Avot* 4:18) states that it is futile to try and comfort others when they are furious or outraged, as they are incapable of listening and reasoning clearly. The Talmud states that one who becomes angry is virtually committing idolatry; either one *controls oneself*, or one becomes *controlled* by something else. The *Zohar* remarks that during consuming moments of rage, it is as if one is under the spell of the "drug of death."

Perhaps audaciously, the Talmud (*Berakhot* 7a) discusses what God asks for during God's own prayers. God's first prayer is, "Let it be My will that My mercy will conquer My anger."

HEARING YOUR OWN VOICE

1. The Mishnah of *Pirkei Avot* (5:11) cites four types of personalities:

   - Easy to become angry and easy to be pacified
   - Hard to become angry and hard to be pacified
   - Hard to become angry and easy to be pacified
   - Easy to become angry and hard to be pacified

   Which type are you? Do you know anyone who fits the third category?

2. The seventh blessing of the *Amidah* (silent standing prayer) can be understood as a request to be granted the strength not to be come upset over the countless, though minute, irritating moments during the day. How can this be achieved?

3. Have you ever shown a "face of anger" while remaining calm within? What enabled you to control yourself?

4. *Ayeka?* What advice would you give yourself to become more patient and compassionate?

Seuda Shlishit

Learning How to Die

This week's *parsha*, *Chukkat*, deals with the mystery of death.

The great Hasidic masters approached the moment of passing without panic or fear.

> When the hour arrived for Rabbi Simcha Bunam from Psyshcha to depart from the world, his wife stood by his bedside and wept bitterly. He said to her, "Be silent – why do you cry? My whole life was only that I might learn how to die."
>
> On the day of his death, the Ba'al Shem Tov told his followers, "I am not worried about myself, for I know clearly that I shall go from this door and immediately enter another door." He sat down on his bed and told his students to stand around him. He prayed with great concentration and devotion, until the syllables of his words could no longer be distinguished. He told them to cover him with blankets and began to shake and tremble as he used to do when he prayed the Silent Prayer. Little by little he grew quiet. They waited until they saw that he had begun his journey through the next door.
>
> Before his death, Rabbi Abraham Joshua Heschel from Apt moaned bitterly over the exile of his people and over the fact

that the Messiah had tarried in coming. Finally he cried out, "The Rabbi of Berditchev said before he died that when he arrived up there he would not rest nor be silent, nor would he allow any of the holy ones to rest or be silent until the Messiah would come. But when he came there, the beauties and wonders of heaven overwhelmed him, so that he forgot about this. But I," concluded the Rabbi of Apt, "I shall not forget."

Rabbi Sussya from Plozk raised his head at midnight and recited the verse "At midnight I rise to praise You," and with these words his soul departed from him.

HEARING YOUR OWN VOICE

1. What do you think that Rabbi Simcha Bunam of Psyshcha meant by "My whole life was only that I might learn how to die?"
2. The Ba'al Shem Tov told his followers, "I am not worried about myself, for I know clearly that I shall go from this door and immediately enter another door." How do you think that this understanding of death might affect the way in which one lives?
3. Do you know anyone who is not afraid of the mystery of death?
4. *Ayeka?* What does the expression "mystery of death" evoke for you?

Balak

A Contentious Witness

This week's *parsha, Balak,* is arguably the most unusual story in the whole Torah. Its primary figures include two non-Jews – Balak, the king of Mo'ab, and Bila'am, the leader and spiritual force of Midyan – as well as Bila'am's mule, who both talks and sees angels. The *parsha* does not impart Jewish law, and virtually no active role is taken either by individual Jews or the Jewish nation.

What is the message of this *parsha*? What eternal struggle is being depicted here? Furthermore, why does this struggle occur precisely at this moment in the travels of the Jewish people?

The book of *Bamidbar* chronicles the growth of the Jewish people from their second to their fortieth year in the desert. It describes a journey from childhood to adulthood, from dependence to independence. Last week's *parsha, Chukkat,* recounted the deaths of Miriam and Aaron. The Jewish people were aware that Moses would not bring them into the Promised Land, and thus soon they would be utterly bereft of the leaders who brought them out of Egypt and nurtured them during their forty years in the desert. Their present condition seemed full of confusion and vulnerability. They had already suffered a multitude of crises, including having been misled by those in positions of authority (the spies) and being witness to a failed rebellion (*Korach*). Soon, upon leaving the desert, their existence would be drastically transformed; no longer would they be graced with the *manna* from heaven or God's unambiguous presence. What would give them the strength to carry on?

In this *parsha*, Balak, the king of Mo'ab, is nervous over the impending approach of the Jewish people. He has previously witnessed the Jewish people request to pass through the land of the Emorites on their way to the Promised Land. Sichon, the Emorite king, denied them passage and launched war against them. In the ensuing battle, he and his people were conclusively defeated. Though the Jewish people harbored no intentions of conquering Mo'ab, their previous victory worried Balak. Concerned that he did not possess the military resources to defeat the Jewish people, he summoned Bila'am to weaken them through his power of speech. "Please come now and curse this people for me, for they are too mighty for me. Perhaps together we may defeat them, and I [Balak] will drive them out of the land, for I know that whomever you [Bila'am] bless will be blessed, and whomever you curse will be cursed" (Numbers 22:6).

Bila'am complied with Balak's request and attempted to denounce the Jews. Yet each time he opened his mouth, only blessings came forth. Three separate times Bila'am disappointed Balak with his words of praise for the Jewish people:

> Who can count the dust of Jacob, and number a quarter of Israel? Let me die the death of the righteous, and let my last end be like his [Jacob's]. (Numbers 23:10)

> God has not beheld iniquity in Jacob nor has He seen perverseness in Israel, the Lord his God is with him, and the trumpet blast of a king is among them.... Behold, the people will rise up as a great lion, and lift up itself as a young lion; it will not lie down until it eats of the prey. (Numbers 23:21, 24)

> How goodly are your tents, Jacob, and your dwellings, Israel.
> Like the winding brooks, like gardens by the river's side, like
> aloes which the Lord has planted, and cedar trees beside the
> waters ... it will eat up the nations, its enemies, and will break
> their bones, and pierce them through with its arrows. It lies
> down like a lion, and like a great lion, who will stir him up?
> Blessed is he that blesses you, and cursed is he that curses you.
> (Numbers 24:5–9)

The story of Bila'am comes to clarify to the Jewish people who
they truly are and what singular powers they possess. Testimony,
conceptually and legally, is suspect when it comes from someone
who has a vested interest in giving it. Thus, according to Jewish
law, relatives may not serve as witnesses for each other. Only when
the witness will not stand to personally benefit from his or her
testimony is it most likely to be totally valid and truthful. Bila'am
was offered riches and honor from Balak to denounce the Jewish
people. Yet, as Bila'am himself stated, "[it is] the word that God
puts into my mouth, that I shall speak" (Numbers 22:38).

Ironically, precisely because of his evil character and intentions,
the praise that he eventually uttered is regarded as being thoroughly
impartial and truthful. Bila'am had no vested interest in praising
the Jewish people. Only his utterances could truly convey to the
Jewish people their power and righteousness. His words, "How
goodly are your tents, Jacob, and your dwellings, Israel," have been
incorporated into the daily prayerbook. In the midst of the confusion and vulnerability of the Jewish people, who faced the daunting
prospect of becoming independent, comes the voice of Bila'am
to remind them of their remarkable gifts, blessings, and potential.

HEARING YOUR OWN VOICE

1. In rabbinic literature, despite the fact that Bila'am praised the Jewish people, he is portrayed very negatively. The Mishnah (*Pirkei Avot* 5:19) counts him among the four individuals who forfeited their place in the world to come (*Sanhedrin* 10:2). How would you judge him?

2. The Mishnah attributes three qualities to Bila'am: "an evil eye, a haughty temperament, and an insatiable spirit." In contrast, Abraham is said to demonstrate "a good eye, a modest temperament, and a humble spirit." Bila'am was clearly blessed with spiritual powers, yet he could not direct them positively. Do you think that it is unusual for someone to be spiritually gifted yet not righteous? What advice or education would you have given to Bila'am?

3. Did you ever learn something positive about yourself from what an adversary of yours said about you?

4. *Ayeka?* Who do you think is the Bila'am of today? What can you learn from him/her?

Shabbat Lunch

Temptation

In this week's *parsha*, Balak, the king of Mo'ab, entreats Bila'am to curse the Jewish people for him. He implores Bila'am, saying, "Let nothing I pray, hinder your coming to me, for I will give you great honor, and anything that you say to me I will do; please come and curse this people for me" (Numbers 22:16–17). Bila'am could not resist Balak's invitation; the temptation of honor and wealth precluded any possibility of refusal.

Who is the guilty party here? The person who tempted or the person who actually committed the crime?

Judaism affirms, "An individual cannot claim that he was just a messenger perpetrating the transgression" (*Bava Kamma* 79a). The one who actually commits the violation is held responsible, and cannot contend that he was simply following orders. Each human being possesses free will and is consequently held accountable for his actions.

Nevertheless, is the one who tempts completely innocent? Isn't he also responsible for the eventual outcome of his suggestion or request?

An answer can be found in the Torah's prohibition against placing a "stumbling block before the blind" (Leviticus 19:14). What exactly is a "stumbling block"? Is the verse talking only about someone who is physically blind?

The commentators extend the "blind" person in the verse to include two additional categories: "blindness of the mind" and "blindness of the heart."

"Blindness of the mind" refers to someone who is lacking in a particular area of knowledge – that is, who is blind regarding a certain matter. "Not putting a stumbling block in front of the blind" thus becomes an injunction against giving improper advice. The Midrash relates that if a person is not financially astute, one should not encourage him to sell his belongings so that one can then purchase them. Similarly, if someone asks for advice concerning a potential spouse, one should not assure him or her that the spouse is appropriate if he or she is not. Both these things are considered to be placing a stumbling block before the blind.

"Blindness of the heart" applies to a person who possesses the requisite information, yet who is still *blinded by an uncontrollable desire*. Thus the biblical prohibition against placing a stumbling block before the blind would admonish us against offering food or drink to someone who may not have the willpower to resist. Similarly, one should not lend money without witnesses, lest the borrower be tempted to deny the transaction.

If people do, in fact, fail because a "stumbling block" was placed in front of them, Jewish law rejects the claim of "I didn't force them; they're adults and they decided for themselves." Precisely because we are human and have weaknesses, we are obligated to help each other overcome "blind spots." Nevertheless, there is no punishment for one who transgresses this injunction. No judge or observer can ever really know what was the true intention behind the bad advice, since the person who gave the advice can always (falsely) assert, "I really had his best interests in mind."

The prohibition against placing a stumbling block comes to remind us that we are ultimately held accountable not only for our actions, but for our words, and not only for our words but also for our intentions.

HEARING YOUR OWN VOICE

1. The verse that prohibits placing a stumbling block before the blind begins, "You should not curse the deaf." Why not? Who really suffers? Is there a connection between the two parts of this verse?

2. Applications of the "stumbling block" principle range from the need for clear traffic signs to the restriction of weapons sales nations that cannot be trusted to control them. The field of advertising is especially vulnerable to violations of "putting a stumbling block in front of the blind." Why? Can you think of ramifications of this principle in business, political life, or contemporary society?

3. Have you ever struggled with the sincerity of the advice that you were giving? How did you clarify to yourself that it was truly for the benefit of the receiver?

4. *Ayeka?* What was the last "stumbling block" that was placed in your path?

Seuda Shlishit

Solitary Meditation

It is a people that shall dwell alone. (Numbers 23:9)

The non-Jewish prophet Bila'am declared that the Jewish people would forever remain separate from the other nations of the world. Their destiny is to remain singularly alone. Is it a blessing or a curse to be alone?

The Hasidic leader Rebbe Nachman of Bratslav wrote extensively of the spiritual value of spending time alone. He insisted that in order to become closer to God, one had to undergo a process of *hitbodedut*, of being alone with oneself. "The only way to fully move beyond one's self and ego, and to become capable of talking directly to God, is through *hitbodedut*." Still today, the essential prayer experience of the Bratslav hasidim takes place in solitude.

Rebbe Nachman wrote of three primary criteria for successful *hitbodedut*:

> Time. The essence of *hitbodedut* is at night, when people can free themselves from concerns of this-worldly matters. Even if one thinks that he or she can find moments of focus during the day, the pressures and nonspiritual pulse of the world necessarily impinge upon concentration.

Location. Moments of *hitbodedut* must occur in a special place, outside of populated areas. Even if a person is alone, the effect of being in a place where others have been recently will disturb the purity and intensity of the *hitbodedut*.

Outpouring of one's heart. In *hitbodedut*, one must sincerely and unreservedly open one's heart. Rebbe Nachman notes several stages in this process. An individual should begin simply by trying to talk with God and should not despair if he or she manages only to say a word or two. One should wait and persist in the *hitbodedut* until the effect of being alone in a special place enables one to begin to talk about one's self, one's life, and one's desires. Eventually, this process of speaking moves the individual to an awareness that is beyond speech. Then, in a special place, alone, in silence, one can become, in the words of Rebbe Nachman, "wholly at one with the source of all reality."

HEARING YOUR OWN VOICE

1. A.B. Yehoshua, contemporary Israeli author and winner of the Israeli prize for literature, takes issue with the value of Jewish separatism. He writes that "The need to find difference must be gotten rid of once and for all.... I repeat this simple truth, that the Jewish people is a people like all peoples, and am astonished to discover to what extent it does not appear simple to many.... We must grab hold of this deep-lying notion [of being different] and slowly try to root it out" (*Between Right and Right,* 1982). Do you think that it is possible and/or advantageous to "root out" the separation between the Jewish people and the other nations?

2. Rebbe Nachman describes the importance of finding special times and places to achieve a state of aloneness. What special time of day or place would you choose to foster a "spiritual conversation"? Have you ever experienced a moment of *hitbodedut* like he describes?

3. What do you think are the advantages of meditation? The disadvantages?

4. *Ayeka?* What small step could you take to bring more quiet time and moments of solitude and reflection into your life?

Pinchas

A Covenant of Broken Peace

Bila'am, the main figure in last week's *parsha*, did not succeed in cursing the Jewish people. To the chagrin of Balak, the king of Mo'ab, who repeatedly implored Bila'am to denounce the Jewish people, words of praise continually sprang forth from Bila'am's mouth. Nevertheless, at the very end of last week's *parsha*, the Jewish people are finally entrapped by the sexual promiscuity and idolatry of Mo'ab, "and the people began to commit harlotry with the daughters of Mo'ab. And they called the people to the sacrifices of their gods, and the people ate, and bowed down to their gods" (Numbers 25:1–2). Tens of thousands of Jews are involved in this behavior and incur the wrath of God.

This week's *parsha* opens with God bestowing a "covenant of peace" upon Pinchas: "And the Lord spoke to Moses, saying, 'Pinchas, the son of Elazar, the son of Aaron the priest, has turned My wrath away from the children of Israel, in that he was *zealous* for My sake among them.... Behold, I give to him My *covenant of peace* (*brit shalom*), and he shall have it, and his seed after him, the covenant of an everlasting priesthood; because he was *zealous* for

304